Introduction to Linear Models

Patrick R. McMullen
Wake Forest University
ISBN: 9798862133431

Introduction

This book was organized to assist graduate students with understanding linear models via a short-course. Specifically, simple linear regression, multiple linear regression and forecasting are covered here. Additionally, chapters on Decision Analysis and Mathematical Programming are included to round-out a short-course relevant to linear models. Chapters from a larger, more general statistics book were extracted and modified accordingly – this was done to keep costs down.

The book references several data sets which are available to the students.

Contents

1. Simple Linear Regression

You have been exposed to the basic foundations of statistical inference – testing a claim via a formal test, so that we can properly articulate our findings to the skeptical scientific community. This is an important accomplishment. This chapter will build on our ability to do this via exploring potential relationships between variables. We read about exploration between variables in everyday life. For example, we have learned about a relationship between exposure to asbestos and mesothelioma, a type of lung cancer. We have learned about a relationship between the amount of time a child watches television and the likelihood of that child being obese.

These "relationships" are typically implied using very subtle language. Nevertheless, these relationships are almost always determined via some form of linear regression – formally exploring the relationships between variables, or entities. In this chapter, we will cover simple linear regression, which is the exploration between two variables. Many informative and important investigations can be made with just a basic understanding of this powerful tool.

1.1 Slope and Intercept

Prior to delving into regression from a statistical standpoint, it is important for us to recall from high school algebra the formula for a line. The lines has two major components: an **intercept** and a **slope**. The reference system for a line is the Cartesian Coordinate System, where "x" represents the horizontal axis and "y" represents the vertical axis. A point in this coordinate system is represented via "(x, y)" notation. The line has the general formula:

$$y = a + bx \hspace{3cm} \text{EQ 1-1}$$

Under this scenario, we assume the x-value is pre-determined – we call "x" an **independent variable**. We assume that y-values are determined by the x values – we call "y" a **dependent variable**.

The intercept, represented by "a" is the value of the y-value when "x" equals zero. Graphically, this is where the line crosses the vertical axis (y-axis). The slope, represented by "b" is the ratio of the change in y to each unit change in *x*. Mathematically, this is often stated as follows:

$$b = \Delta y\ /\ \Delta x$$

EQ 1-2

Figure 1-1 shows a line of the form "*y* = 3 + 2*x*.

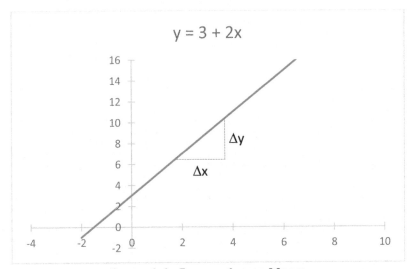

FIGURE 1-1. EXAMPLE LINEAR MODEL

This example line has an intercept of "3" – notice how the line crosses the vertical axis at *y* = 3 (*y* = 3 + 2(0) = 3). This example line has a slope of "2." The $\Delta y\ /\ \Delta x$ ratio is equal to "2" – this is detailed in the "wedged" section of Figure 1-1.

1.2 Ordinary Least Squares Regression

In statistics, we are given a set of data and it is our job to "fit" a line through the points represented by the data set. As an example of a data set, consider a situation where we are interested in exploring the relationship between price and demand of a product. In this example, we have randomly visited convenience stores in Winston-Salem, NC. In each store, we looked at the price of a 12-pack of Diet Dr. Pepper in cans. Management provided us with the sales data for this product in units sold for the previous week. This data set is as follows:

Pr.	3.38	3.42	3.48	3.52	3.55	3.55	3.61	3.61	3.67	3.72
Dem	83	86	83	81	81	83	81	81	80	80

TABLE 1-1. PRICE VS DEMAND DATA FOR DIET DR. PEPPER PROBLEM

A scatter plot is shown in Figure 1-2.

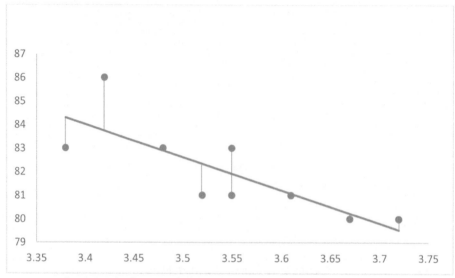

FIGURE 1-2. SCATTER PLOT FOR DIET DR. PEPPER DEMAND DATA

Here we see points, showing the demand for each price, as the result of our random sampling effort. As one might expect, there seems to be an inverse relationship between price and demand – as price increases, demand seems to increase.

In order to find the "best" line relating price to demand, we select a slope and intercept that minimizes the **sum of squared errors**. Figure 1-2 also shows a fitted line. This fitted line is the result of selecting a slope and intercept that minimizes the total squared difference between the actual data points and the fitted line. These error terms are shown via the thin vertical lines spanning the fitted line and the actual data values. We square these error terms for two reasons: first, to prevent negative numbers; second, to amplify large errors. Statistical software will provide us with a slope and intercept value that minimizes the sum of squared errors. The practice of finding the slope and intercept terms is called "**ordinary least squares regression.**"

The next section will detail how to perform ordinary least squares regression in Microsoft Excel, but for our data set, we have a slope of -$14.00 and an intercept of 131.60 units of Diet Dr. Pepper. What this means is that when the price is zero, we can expect a demand of 131.60 units. This result, of course, should not be taken literally, but the intercept is where the line crosses the vertical ("y") axis. The slope tells is that for each $1 increase in the price, we can expect demand to *decrease* 14.00 units. The negative sign tells us it is a decrease.

1.3 Statistical Inference for Slope and Intercept

Here, we continue with our Diet Dr. Pepper example and learn how to use Excel to give us the slope and intercept. Then we test the statistical significance of the slope and intercept.

1.3.1   Excel for Regression

In order to learn the values of the slope and intercept, we use the Data Analysis Tools | Regression option. We enter the data associated with the "x" and "y" values. Again, for our example, Price is the "x" variable, and Demand is the "y" variable. We specify an output range and then "run the regression." We get a very comprehensive output report. Selected output is shown in Table 1-2.

	Coefficients	Standard Error	t Stat	P-value
Intercept	131.60	12.98	10.14	< 0.0001
Price	-14.00	3.65	-3.83	0.0050

TABLE 1-2. SLOPE AND INTERCEPT FOR DIET DR. PEPPER DATA SET

The table shows the slope and intercept values that we learned earlier. The other presented data is discussed next.

1.3.2   Testing the Slope and Intercept

Now that we know the values of the slope and intercept, we need to address the question as to whether or not they are statistically significant. To do this, we first present the linear model relating "x" and "y" for an entire population:

$$Y = \alpha + \beta X \qquad \text{EQ 1-3}$$

Here, the "x" and "y" terms are capitalized to imply data from the entire population. This equation shows "α," which represents the intercept for the population[1], while "β" represents the slope for the population. We need to test the slope and intercept for statistical significance. These hypotheses are as follows:

$$H_0\!: \ \alpha = 0; \ H_A\!: \ \alpha \neq 0 \qquad \text{EQ 1-4}$$

$$H_0\!: \ \beta = 0; \ H_A\!: \ \beta \neq 0 \qquad \text{EQ 1-5}$$

Eq 1-4 is a test for the significance of the intercept, while Eq **1-5** is a test for the significance of the slope. The test for the intercept is not of importance here – the intercept is important in terms of minimizing the sum of squared error value, but for this book, the statistical significance of the intercept is not a matter of concern. What is important, however, is the test for the statistical significance of the slope. In Eq **1-5**, the H_0 states that the slope is equal to zero. This means that as X changes, Y does not change – Y is not sensitive to X. The H_A says that the slope is not equal to zero, meaning that as X changes, Y changes as well – Y is sensitive to X.

These tests for the significance of the slope and intercept are always as presented in these two equations. They are always two-tailed tests. Because of this consistency, we never have to formally state them – they are always the same. This provides Excel, or whatever software is being used to present us the appropriate statistics to interpret. We have to, of course, compare these hypothesized values to the estimated values, which we know to be "a" for the intercept and "b" for the slope. The test statistic for the intercept is as follows:

$$t = \frac{a - \alpha}{se_a} = \frac{a - 0}{se_a} = \frac{a}{se_a} \qquad \text{EQ 1-6}$$

---

[1] Not to be confused with the level of significance as covered previously. These two entities are independent from each other.

The test statistic for the slope is as follows:

$$t = \frac{b - \beta}{se_b} = \frac{b - 0}{se_b} = \frac{b}{se_b}$$

EQ 1-7

Because both α and β are hypothesized to be zero, we substitute zero into both equations above, and we end up with the "estimates" of the intercept (a) and slope (b) divided by their standard errors. The end result is the two t-statistics above very closely resemble the t-statistics we used in the Statistical Inference / Hypothesis Testing chapter.

The results of these two-tailed tests are also shown in Table 1-2. Slope and Intercept for Diet Dr. Pepper Data Set. When the estimates of the slope and intercept are divided by their standard errors, we have the appropriate t-statistics and p-values. You will notice that the p-value associated with the intercept is < 0.0001. Here, we reject the H_0, and claim the intercept is statistically significant. The t-statistic associated with the slope term is -3.83, with an associated p-value of 0.0050. This tells us that the relationship between Demand and Price is statistically significant – there is a meaningful relationship between price and demand.

1.4 Estimation / Prediction

Let's continue with our Diet Dr. Pepper example and assume that we are satisfied with the belief that Price and Demand have a statistically significant relationship. We can then use the following equation to estimate Demand given some pre-specified or pre-determined Price:

Demand = 131.60 – 14.00(Price)   EQ 1-8

Given this relationship, however, we need to be careful of the values of Price we use to estimate demand. This model was constructed using a minimum Price of $3.38 and a maximum value of $3.72. Because of this, we can only use this model to estimate Demand for values of price in this interval. If we fail to do this, we are, in essence, "extrapolating," which is a pretentious term for "guessing." As such, we should only estimate for values of "x" that are between x_{min} and x_{max}.

There is one other statistic worth discussing, which is the R^2 value. The value of R^2 tells us the percent of variation in our "y" variable that is explained by our "x" variable. This measure of R^2 is essentially a measure of the model's predictive ability. The R^2 value can be as low as zero, and as high as one. We want our R^2 value to be as high as possible, as that would maximize the percent variation in "y" that is explained by "x." For our example problem, the R^2 value is 0.6473. This value is also included with our Excel output. This means that 64.73% of the variation in Demand is explained by Price. This implies, then, that 35.27% of the variation in Demand has not been explained. As such, when using this model for prediction purposes, we should temper our expectations on the quality of our predictive ability, because much of the variation in demand is explained by entities other than price.

1.5 Conclusions

As stated at the beginning of this chapter, linear regression is the study of relationships among variables. This means that our paramount interest is to see if two variables are related. If they are related – meaning we reject the H_0 regarding a slope of zero – then, and one then, can we pursue the topic of prediction. In short, significance is more important than prediction.

With multiple linear regression – using multiple independent variables ("x" variables), we have the ability to increase our predictive ability via increasing the R^2 value associated with a model.

For now, however, it is most important to understand that simple linear regression is mainly concerned about whether or not variables are related, while multiple linear regression is most concerned about optimizing the predictive ability of our model.

1.6 Exercises

1.   Earlier in this chapter, while talking about the Diet Dr. Pepper example, I mentioned that if we increased the sample size, we would decrease the p-value associated with the slope term. Why is this the case?

2.   Let us visit the "ExamScores" data set. This data set has two columns: the "Exam 1" column is the Exam 1 score for a specific student. The "Exam 2" column is the Exam 2 score for the same student. Explain how simple linear regression could be used as a tool to study the student's propensity for success.

3. Using the "ExamScores" data set, are Exam 1 scores and Exam 2 scores related?

4. Using the "ExamScores" data set, report the R^2 term with the Exam 1 score as the independent variable and the Exam 2 score as the dependent variable.

5. Using the "ExamScores" data set, report the R^2 term with the Exam 2 score as the independent variable and the Exam 1 score as the dependent variable.

6. How do you reconcile your results from the above two questions?

7. Using the "ExamScores" data set, what score would you expect a student to get on Exam 2 if they got an 83 on Exam 1?

8. Using the "NewspaperAdvertisements" data set, report on the relationship between Ads/Month and Customers/Month. Is the relationship meaningful?

9. Using the "NewspaperAdvertisements" data set, estimate customers visiting the store per month when 15 advertisements were made for a specific month. Are you comfortable with this estimate? Why or why not?

10. Using the "NewspaperAdvertisements" data set, estimate customers visiting the store per month when 23 advertisements were made for a specific month. Are you comfortable with this estimate? Why or why not?

11. Using the "NewspaperAdvertisements" data set, what is the predictive ability of this model?

12. Using the "BaseballSalaries2014" data set, report on the relationship between the team payroll and winning percentage. Is the relationship meaningful? Do these results surprise you? Why or why not?

13. Using the "BaseballSalaries2014" data set, estimate a team's winning percentage with an annual payroll of $150M. Are you comfortable with this estimate? Why or why not?

14. Using the "BaseballSalaries2014" data set, estimate a team's winning

percentage with an annual payroll of $300M. Are you comfortable with this estimate? Why or why not?

15. Using the "BaseballSalaries2014" data set, describe the predictive ability of your model.

16. Look at the two regression plots below. For each plot, the ordinary least squares regression line is fitted through the data. Of the two plots, which one has the higher R^2 value. Justify your response.

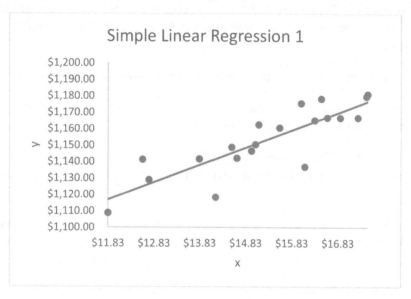

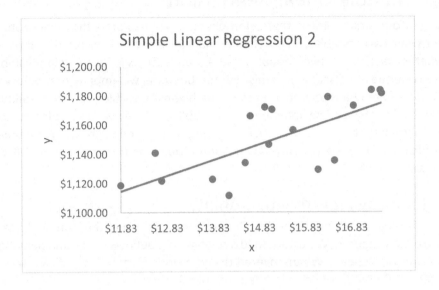

2. Multiple Linear Regression

In our simple linear regression chapter, we explored the relationship between two variables. This chapter had an emphasis on relationships – whether or not the two variables had a statistically significant relationship. We continue our discussion in this chapter, but here, we emphasize predictive ability – finding a model that gives us the highest possible predictive ability. We do this by adding independent variables, which we also refer to as **predictor variables**. The practice of studying such relationships when multiple predictor variables are involved is called **multiple linear regression** or "MLR" for short.

2.1 Improving Predictive Ability

Let us recall our Diet Dr. Pepper example from the simple linear regression chapter. We established a relationship between price and demand for Diet Dr. Pepper. We discovered that the slope term was significant (t = -3.90, p = 0.0045). We also learned that our R^2 term was 0.6473 – 64.73% of the variation in Demand is explained by Price. This means that 35.27% (1 - 0.6473) of the variation in Demand is explained by something other than Price. If we are interested in estimating or predicting Demand, it seems that we'd like more predictive ability.

2.1.1   Adding More Variables

More predictive ability can be obtained if we add more predictor (independent) variables to our model. This can be done quite easily in Excel – when we are asked for the "X" variables, we simply "paint" all of the independent variables.[2]

Let us continue our Diet Dr. Pepper example from the Simple Linear Regression chapter. This time, however, we will add a predictor variable "Advertising," which represents the number of signs advertising the Diet Dr. Pepper. The advertising is done in the proximity of the store. The new data set, then, is as follows:

---

[2] To "paint" the necessary predictor variables, they must be in adjacent columns. Otherwise, Excel cannot process them. Columns of predictor variables in non-adjacent columns will not work in Excel.

Price	3.38	3.42	3.48	3.52	3.55	3.55	3.61	3.61	3.67	3.72
Adv.	28	30	28	26	26	28	26	26	26	27
Dem.	83	86	83	81	81	83	81	81	80	80

TABLE 2- 1. PRICE AND ADVERTISING VS. DEMAND DATA FOR DIET DR. PEPPER

We then ask Excel to perform the linear regression. This time, however, we make certain that both Price and Advertising are treated as "x" variables.

2.1.2   F-Statistic and Regression Output

Prior to discussing the regression output of the example problem, it is appropriate for us to address the hypothesis testing associated with multiple linear regression. When examining the output, the first thing one should consider is the general set of hypotheses that accompany such analyses. The null and alternative hypotheses are as follows:

H_0: The independent variables are not related to
the dependent variable

H_A: The independent variables are related to the
dependent variable

EQ. 2- 1

The hypotheses stated above are always the case. As such, there is no need to explicitly define them.

To determine whether or not to reject the H_0, we examine the following statistic, which we refer to as the "F-statistic."

$$F = \frac{Explained\ Variation}{Unexplained\ Variation}$$

EQ. 2- 2

This statistic should not look entirely unfamiliar. We saw something very similar when we discussed the Analysis of Variance. If this ratio is high (the associated p-value being less than some threshold value, such as 0.05), we reject the H_0 and claim that there is a meaningful relationship between the independent and dependent variables.[3]

---

[3] In truth, the significance of the F-statistic in multiple linear regression almost always shows significance, because we are trying to optimize the predictive ability, which

For our example problem, our F-statistic is 46.30, with an associated p-value of < 0.0001. Therefore, both Price and Advertising have a meaningful relationship with Demand.

The next order of business is to determine whether or not our predictor variables are statistically significant. Selected regression output is shown in Table 2-2.

	Coefficients	Standard Error	t Stat	P-value
Intercept	78.89	11.71	6.74	0.0003
Price	-6.29	2.27	-2.77	0.0276
Advertisement	0.94	0.18	5.30	0.0011

TABLE 2- 2. INTERCEPT AND SLOPES FOR MLR DIET DR. PEPPER PROBLEM

Here we see that the intercept and both slope terms are statistically significant – all p-values are very small. You will also notice that the values of the intercept and the Price slope have changed from the simple linear regression ("SLR") problem. This should not be a surprise, because with the addition of the new term (Advertisement) all other terms will have new values in the pursuit of minimizing the sum of squared errors term.

Now that we can take comfort in that we have a meaningful relationship between Demand and the predictor variables of Price and Advertisements, we can turn our attention to prediction. Excel tells us that our R^2 value is 0.9297. This means that 92.97% of the variation in Demand is explained by both Price and Advertisements. This is a great improvement over the R^2 value from our earlier model, where Price was the only predictor variable for Demand. In general, adding predictor variables to a linear regression will result in an increase in R^2. As such, adding variables to a model improves our predictive ability.

We can now predict Demand by using the predictors of Price and Advertisements via the following equation:

$$\text{Demand} = 78.89 - (6.29)(\text{Price}) + (0.94)(\text{Advertisements})$$ EQ. 2- 3

---

strongly implies a significant relationship between the "x" and "y" variables already exists.

We must, however, bear in mind that when predicting; make sure we use values of the predictor variables that are in range of the values from our data set. Otherwise, we are extrapolating, which can provide unreliable results.

2.2 Multicollinearity

Let us consider another example, where I am interested in estimating GMAT Score using the predictor variables of undergraduate GPA and Hours Studying for the GMAT exam. This sounds like a reasonable experiment. It seems reasonable to expect that as both undergraduate GPA and Hours Studying increase, so would the associated GMAT score.

To further investigate this, the data set "GMATExample" has been provided. When performing a multiple linear regression where GMAT score is the dependent (response variable), and GPA and Hours Studying are the predictor variables, we have an F-statistic of 824.93, with an associated p-value < 0.0001. We also have an R^2 value of 0.6238. So far, so good.

When we look at the statistical significance of the individual predictor variables, however, we have the following:

	Coefficients	Standard Error	t Stat	P-value
Intercept	-255.47	41.80	-6.11	< 0.0001
GPA	205.93	44.25	4.65	< 0.0001
Hours Studying	2.96	2.35	1.26	0.2091

TABLE 2- 3. PREDICTOR VARIABLES FOR GMAT EXAMPLE

When looking at the table above, a problem becomes evident. The slope term for Hours Studying doesn't show statistical significance. We are being told that there is no relationship between Hours Studying and GMAT score. This doesn't make sense. Upon further investigation, a simple linear regression is performed between GMAT score and Hours studying – GPA is excluded from this analysis. This regression reveals that Hours Studying is in fact related to GMAT score (t = 39.94, p < 0.0001).

In summary, multiple linear regression tells us that Hours Studying is not related to GMAT score, while simple linear regression tells us that Hours Studying is related to GMAT score. These conflicting results are a consequence of **multicollinearity** – a strong correlation between predictor variables. While multicollinearity does not have any impact of our ability for prediction, it greatly impedes our ability to interpret individual predictor variables.

2.2.1   Correlation

When we define multicollinearity above, we state that it is the presence of a strong correlation of predictor variables. Now **correlation** must be defined. Correlation is a degree of relationship between variables. That definition sounds eerily familiar – simple linear regression explores relationships between variables. The difference between correlation and simple linear regression is that simple linear regression explains the relationship between slope and intercept, along with the results of associated hypothesis tests, while correlation provides a single standardized statistic describing the relationship between the two variables of interest.

This single standardized statistic used to measure correlation is called the correlation coefficient, ρ. This value of ρ is always in the interval ($-1 \leq \rho \leq 1$). This value of ρ, intended to measure the correlation between "x" and "y," is determined as follows:

$$\rho = \frac{\sum_{i=1}^{n}(x_i - \bar{x})(y_i - \bar{y})}{\sqrt{\sum_{i=1}^{n}(x_i - \bar{x})^2/(n-1)} \sqrt{\sum_{i=1}^{n}(y_i - \bar{y})^2/(n-1)}} \qquad \text{EQ. 2-4}$$

Fortunately, this value is calculated for us using the "=correl(*range1, range2*)" function in Excel. Of greater value, however, is the use of the correlation matrix tool available in the Data Analysis Tools. The correlation matrix tool will provide an entire matrix of pairwise correlations between all variables selected. Using this tool for the data in our problem, we have the following:

	GMAT Score	GPA	Hours Studying
GMAT Score	1		
GPA	0.7894	1	
Hours Studying	0.7846	0.9894	1

TABLE 2-4 .CORRELATION MATRIX FOR GMAT SCORE EXAMPLE PROBLEM

2.2.2   Remediation

If we take a close look at our correlation matrix above, we see that we have also included the response variable of GMAT Score. This will be discussed further momentarily. For now, you should take notice of the correlation of 0.9894 – the standardized relationship between the two predictor variables, GPA and hours studying. This means that Hours Studying and GPA are essentially telling us the same thing. Because of this, we have multicollinearity, and when two predictors are highly correlated, our regression output can be counterintuitive. Such is the case here – our multiple regression output tells us that Hours Studying *is not* meaningful, when simple regression tells us Hours Studying *is* meaningful.

What do we do when we get conflicting results like this? There are many opinions on this matter, but I strongly prefer the most **parsimonious** approach. I prefer to remove one of the correlated variables, and let it be explained by the remaining variable. In this situation, it makes the most sense to remove Hours Studying and let it be explained by GPA, because its correlation with GMAT score (the response variable) is less than GPA's correlation with GMAT score (0.7846 < 0.7894).

Because we have removed Hours Studying and let it be explained by GPA, our model reduces to GMAT score as the dependent variable, and with only GPA as our independent variable.

2.3 Parsimony

With having only one predictor variable now, we once again perform a linear regression without Hours Studying as a predictor variable. The results are as follows:

	Coefficients	Std. Error	t Stat	P-value
Intercept	-302.03	19.36	-15.60	< 0.0001
GPA	260.96	6.43	40.59	< 0.0001

TABLE 2- 5. GMAT SCORE AS A FUNCTION OF GPA ONLY

Of course, the lone slope of GPA is highly significant (t = 40.59, p < 0.0001). Most importantly, however, is the R^2 value, which is 0.6232 – 62.32% of the variation in GMAT score is explained by GPA. Comparing that to the multiple regression model, where GMAT score is explained by GPA and Hours studying, we have an R^2 of 0.6238. In other words, by removing Hours Studying from our model, we only lose 0.0006 from our R^2 term. A meaningless loss.

This simple example best illustrates the most important aspect of multiple regression, which is **parsimony**. The word "parsimony" is not used much anymore, but it generally implies thrift.[4] In the context of model-fitting, parsimony is intended to suggest the use of as few variables as possible to get the most predictive model. In our present situation, the model with one predictor variable is far superior to the one with two predictor variables because we get the same predictive power with one less term to "worry" about and/or discuss.

2.4 Conclusions

Simple Linear Regression is a tool to explore whether or not relationships exist between variables. With only a single predictor variable, we would be naïve to assume Simple Linear Regression as a good predictive tool. This is where Multiple Linear Regression comes in. Multiple Linear Regression builds on relationships (uncovered by Simple Linear Regression) and attempts to optimize the predictive fit by adding variables. Those variables, however, should be chosen wisely. When the appropriate variables are added, our R^2 term approaches a value of 1.00, resulting in a good predictive model.

If we choose too many predictor variables, we can still have a good predictive model, but we lose our ability to explain our model in a concise manner. We should always attempt to maximize the R^2 term with as few predictor variables as possible.

2.5 Exercises

1.   A company that delivers equipment is attempting to understand what determines annual maintenance cost for their fleet of their nine trucks. A data set named "TruckMaintainence" is to be used, where data is given for each truck including the annual maintenance cost for each truck, the number of miles on the truck, and the age of the truck in years. Using $\alpha = 0.05$, please address the following:

---

[4] Charles Dickens often used the word "parsimony" in his work. In the Dickensian context, it implies "thrift" – not spending more money than needed. In our work here, it is important not to use more words and/or variables than needed.

a.   Yes or No: is there an overall relationship between the annual maintenance cost of the truck with the predictor variables of mileage of the truck and the age of the truck.

b.   Justify your response above.

c.   Is the current parsimonious? Why or why not?

d.   What is the most parsimonious model? Justify your response.

2.   The data set named "CollegeProbability" contains three variables of data. These variables are "College Prob," "Class Size," and "SAT Score." Definitions of these variables are as follows:

College Prob: this is the probability that the student in question will attend college.

Class Size: this is the number of students from the class in which the student in question comes.

SAT Score: this is the SAT score that the student in question earned.

For example, the very first data point tells us that the student in question has a 63.52% chance of attending college. This particular student came from a class size of 21, and earned a score of 1232 on the SAT test.

Your job for this problem is to find the most parsimonious model that explains the probability of attending college. When finding this model, explain the steps you have taken **without** use of Excel terminology.

3.   We are interested in determining the driving forces behind mutual fund performance.   The attached data set, called "MutualFundPerformance" contains annual return data (in %) for several mutual funds. For each fund, experience (in years) of the mutual fund's manager is provided, along with the fund manager's salary (in $1,000s). The fund type is also provided, which is either a stock fund or bond fund. Using this data, please address the following questions:

a.   Do the experience of the fund manager, the salary of the fund manager, and the fund type have an aggregate relationship with the mutual fund's performance?

b.   Explain the model you used in part "a" above.

23

c. Using the model constructed in part "a" above, estimate the fund's return for a bond fund with a fund manager earning a salary of $200,000/year and 12 years experience?

d. Is multicollinearity a problem? Why or why not?

e. What is the most parsimonious model that should be used to explain the mutual fund's annual return? Justify your response.

4. I have a data set ("MyStockData") which details daily stock prices of MyStock – a stock that I own. I am trying to use three other stocks to analyze and predict the price of MyStock. Using the attached information, along with a value of $\alpha = 0.01$, please address the following questions:

a. Yes or No: do Stocks A, B and C have an aggregate relationship with MyStock?

b. Support your above response.

c. Yes or No: Is multicollinearity a problem?

d. Support your above response.

e. What is the most parsimonious model? Explain your reasoning.

f. If Stocks A, B and C are priced at $35, $17, $86 respectively, what would expect the price of MyStock to be, when using the most parsimonious model?

5. A beer distributor needs to understand the relationship between the response variable of delivery time and the two predictor variables of distance to travel and the number of cases to deliver. This data is provided ("BeerDistributionTime"). Using this data, please answer the following questions:

a. Is there an aggregate relationship between delivery time and the two predictor variables of distance to travel and cases to deliver?

b. Justify your above answer.

c. Is multicollinearity a problem? Why or why not?

d. What is the most parsimonious model? Explain your reasoning.

6. A junior golf tournament was held in Walnut Creek, California. There were 500 participants – all of them boys. These participants ranged in age from as young as 13 to as old as 18. For each participant, their 18-hole score was recorded, along with their handicap (a basic measure of the golfer's skill), age, and the number of hours per week that the golfer of interest practices. This data is included ("JuniorGolfTournament"). Using this information, please address the following:

a.   Do age, handicap and hours/week of practice time have an aggregate relationship with the tournament score? Why or why not?

b.   Which predictor variable has the strongest relationship with score? Explain your rationale.

c.   Is multicollinearity present? Why or why not.

d.   Using the most parsimonious model, estimate the score of a 14-year-old with a handicap of 15 who practices 19 hours/week.

3. Business Forecasting

We now address a topic that technically does not fit into the world of traditional "statistics," but it is part of Quantitative Methods – the very large topic of business forecasting. Business forecasting is where we take historical data and "extrapolate it into the future. With the prediction we did in the Simple Linear Regression and Multiple Linear Regression chapters, we "interpolated." That is, we took data, built a model, and estimated within the boundaries of the data we have. With forecasting, we take data, build a model, and estimate "beyond" the boundaries of the data we have. We estimate what will happen in the future based upon historical data we have gathered and analyzed.

There are many forecasting tools, but we will concentrate on the regression-based tools, given we now have a basic understanding of how the regression tools work.

3.1 Time Series Analysis

We can think of forecasting as "time series analysis." A **time series** is a collection of historical data. This historical data has an observation for some regular time interval, such as daily, weekly, monthly, etc. These time intervals must be evenly spaced for our presented methodology to work properly.

3.2 Simple Forecasting Tools

Prior to our delving into the regression-based forecasting tools, we will briefly cover the simple forecasting tools – the moving average tools, where we simply extrapolate into the future by averaging historical data. We will start by considering the simple time series shown here:

Day	1	2	3	4	5	6	7	8
Demand	12	12	13	15	16	16	19	20

TABLE 3- 1. TIME SERIES DATA FOR SIMPLE PROBLEM

For these problems, we will introduce the terms D_t and F_t, which mean demand for period t and the Forecast for period t.

3.2.1   Simple Moving Average

The simple moving average forecasting approach is the simples approach imaginable. We simple select the most recent past values of demand and average them. The number of periods we select to average is determined by the forecaster. For example we could choose three averaging periods, and the resultant forecast for the next period F_9, would be as follows:

$$F_9 = (D_8 + D_7 + D_6)/3 = (20 + 19 + 16)/3 = 18.33 \qquad \text{EQ 3-1}$$

3.2.2   Weighted Moving Average

One of the unpleasant realities of the Simple Moving Average approach is that each historical period used in the forecast is considered just as important as the others. This may not be appropriate – most recent periods are often considered the most important when forecasting. A weighted moving average might remediate this problem – this is when the forecaster decides how important historical periods are, or how much "weight" historical periods should carry.

For our example problem, we will continue to use the most recent three periods to make our forecast. This time, let's assume the most recent period receives a weight of 0.5, the period prior to that receives a weight of 0.3, and the period prior to that receives a weight of 0.2. Notice these three weights sum to 1. Our forecast then becomes:

$$F_9 = .5D_8 + .3D_7 + .2D_6 = .5(20) + .3(19) + .2(16) = 18.33 \qquad \text{EQ 3-2}$$

This approach can be thought of as an improvement to the simple moving average approach, as the forecaster can customize the relative importance of historical data.

Unfortunately, neither of the forecasting approaches above is reliable. The reason is that whatever value we forecast into the future, that value will always be somewhere between the minimum and maximum values that we use for our average. In short, we are interpolating, when there are times we need to be extrapolating.

3.3.3 Differencing

The concept of differencing enables us to extrapolate, as opposed to interpolate. If we take the difference in demand (or whatever entity we are trying to forecast) from one period and the prior period, and average all of those periodic differences, we have the average change per time unit. If we let "Δ_t, represent the difference between periods t and $t-1$, we have the following:

$$\Delta_t = D_t - D_{t-1} \qquad \qquad \textbf{EQ 3-3}$$

And when these values of Δ_t are averaged across all possible differences, we have an average of difference ($\bar{\Delta}$) determined via the following:

$$\bar{\Delta} = \frac{1}{n-1} \sum_{t=2}^{n} \Delta_t \qquad \qquad \textbf{EQ 3-4}$$

For this notation, n represents the number of periods (or data points) in our time series. Our table below shows the difference for our example time series.

Day	1	2	3	4	5	6	7	8
Demand	12	12	13	15	16	16	19	20
Δ_t		0	1	2	1	0	3	1

TABLE 3- 2. TIME SERIES DATA FOR SIMPLE PROBLEM

We have an average difference of $\bar{\Delta} = 1.14$. This means that we can expect an average increase of 1.14 units for each subsequent time period. This difference measure can be added to the most recent data value we have. As such, we can forecast for period 9: $F_9 = D_8 + \bar{\Delta}$, which is 20 + 1.14 = 21.14. This difference measure can be thought of a simpler version of slope, enabling the difference to be applied into as many future periods as needed.

3.3 Regression-Based Forecasting

Differencing is far better than the moving average approaches, but it nevertheless is naive in that fails to minimize the sum of squared errors, provided by regression. Regression based forecasting can take care of this for us when we exploit the model where demand is a function of the time period. In other words, we treat our time period as the independent variable and we treat our Demand value as the dependent variable. Once we have estimates of slope and intercept, we can "fit" values of demand:

$$\hat{D}_t = \text{Intercept} + \text{Slope}(t) \qquad \text{EQ 3-5}$$

Comparing our values of actual Demand (D_t) with those "fitted," we can calculate the error for each time period, which in forecasting, we call this the absolute deviation (AD_t):

$$AD_t = |D_t - \hat{D}_t| \qquad \text{EQ 3-6}$$

The mean absolute deviation (MAD) is simply the average of the AD_t values for all time periods:

$$MAD = \frac{1}{n}\sum_{t=1}^{n} AD_t \qquad \text{EQ 3-7}$$

Knowing the forecast error (MAD), we can use our "fit" model above to forecast into the future, or "extrapolate."

$$F_t = \text{Intercept} + \text{Slope}(t) \qquad \text{EQ 3-8}$$

3.2.1   Linear Trends

Continuing with the example we used for the other forecasting approaches, simple linear regression forecasting for the data set provides an intercept of 9.96 and a slope of 1.20, or more formally, we can use the following for forecasting into the next period:

$$F_t = 9.96 + 1.20(t) \qquad \text{EQ 3-9}$$

The actual "fits" and absolute deviation values are below:

Day	1	2	3	4	5	6	7	8
D_t	12	12	13	15	16	16	19	20
$\hat{D}_t$	11.17	12.37	13.57	14.77	15.98	17.18	18.38	19.58
AD_t	0.83	0.37	0.57	0.23	0.02	1.18	0.62	0.42

TABLE 3- 3. REGRESSION FORECASTING RESULTS FOR EXAMPLE PROBLEM

Figure 3.1 shows a time series plot of the given data along with the regression forecasting line, where we have forecast two periods into the future (F_9 = 20.79, F_{10} = 21.99).

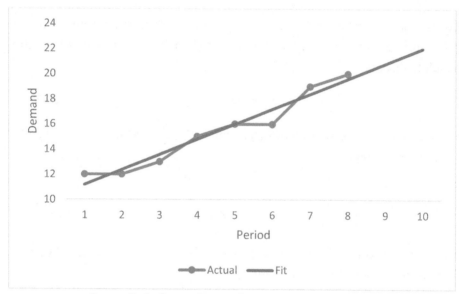

FIGURE 3- 1. SIMPLE LINEAR REGRESSION FORECASTING

One might note how the forecast line is simply a continuation of the trend, which we quantified via the simple linear regression.

3.2.2   Nonlinear Trends

Sometimes our trend is not linear. Consider the data shown in the plot below:

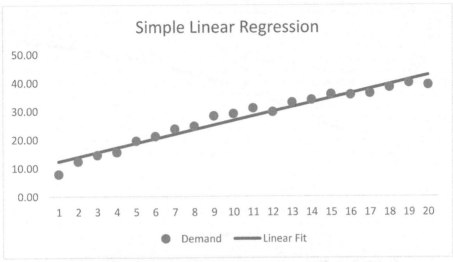

FIGURE 3- 2. NONLINEAR DATA WITH LINEAR FIT ($R^2 = 0.95$).

Upon careful inspection, you might notice that the trend line overestimates the first few periods, underestimates the middle periods, and once again overestimates the latter periods. This suggests that the trend is nonlinear. Perhaps we are "splitting hairs" here, but one can make a very reasonable argument for a nonlinear trend. When this occurs, we can use multiple linear regression as a means to achieve "nonlinear regression." We can do this by creating a new independent variable called t^2, which is simply the period multiplied by itself and used as a predictor variable, resulting in the following general equation:

$$\widehat{D}_t = a + b_1 t + b_2 t^2 \qquad \text{EQ 3- 10}$$

Using multiple regression to estimate the intercept and slope terms, we have the following model we can use for forecasting:

$$\widehat{D}_t = 5.96 + 2.88t - .06t^2 \qquad \text{EQ 3- 11}$$

A time series plot of the fitted model is shown below:

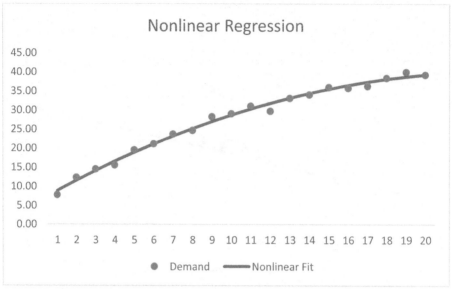

FIGURE 3- 3. NONLINEAR DATA WITH NONLINEAR FIT (R^2 = 0.99)

Two things should be noted from inspection of Figure 3.3. First, notice how the nonlinear fit better captures the data points than does the line via the simple regression model. Second, notice how the associated R^2 term has increased about 4% from the simple regression model.

3.2.3   Microsoft Excel and Forecasting

One of Microsoft Excel's greatest attributes is that it does an excellent job at finding the best fit for a data set. Given a plot of data, right-clicking the mouse button and selecting "Add Trendline" opens up an almost infinite collection of tools to select the best "fit" for the given data set. One can select from a straight line, a polynomial curve, a power curve, a logarithmic curve, an exponential curve, etc. From these choices, there are a variety of parameters to choose from as well. It is worth experimenting with these tools and options to find the best fit. Be warned, however, the principle of parsimony should always apply- always select a model that can be explained. Excel's trendline options are many. This is a very powerful tool. Nevertheless, as powerful as this tool is, performing regression via the Analysis Tools as we have done throughout this book is still needed to determine whether or not the model parameters (slope, etc.) are statistically significant.

3.4 Seasonality in Forecasting

The final forecasting topic we cover is seasonal forecasting. Seasonality exists in almost all forms of commerce. For example, champagne sales are higher than average in December. Retail stores are busy in November and December. More barbeque sauce is sold in the summer months compared to other parts of the year. Tax accountants are very busy in March and April. Maine has lots of tourists in the summer months, while Florida has lots of tourists in the winter months. This list could go on and on, but seasonality is a powerful force of nature. It is important we have the ability to forecast in the presence of seasonality.

This can be accomplished via a variety of tools, but we will use seasonalized time series regression forecasting here. Conceptually, this is a straightforward process. We will illustrate this with an example via a seasonal time series shown in Table 3.4 and Figure 3.4.

Quarter	Period	Year 1 Demand	Period	Year 2 Demand	Period	Year 3 Demand
1	1	85	5	93	9	96
2	2	118	6	130	10	133
3	3	83	7	89	11	95
4	4	69	8	74	12	75

TABLE 3- 4. SEASONAL TIME SERIES DATA

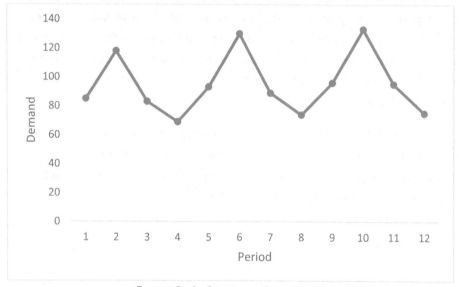

FIGURE 3- 4. SEASONAL TIME SERIES

Table 3.4 show that this time series is organized slightly differently from what we've seen thus far. Each row indicates the "quarter." Each pair of columns indicates the period number and year. The table shows that there are three years of quarterly data, for twelve total observations. Quarters are organized by row, and year is organized by column.

Most importantly, however, Figure 3.4 shows that this time series is in fact seasonal – peaks and valleys are present, and in this specific case, the peaks and valleys repeat themselves every fourth period.

3.4.1   Order of Seasonality

We first need to determine the "order" of seasonality. The order of seasonality is how many individual periods there are for each cycle. If we have monthly data, the order of seasonality is twelve. If we have hourly data, the order of seasonality is twenty-four. For our example, we have quarterly data, so the order of seasonality is four (Figure 4 supports this). The order of seasonality can be determined by either examining a time series plot or by understanding how many time periods there are for each temporal cycle.

Given that we know the order of seasonality for our problem is four, we compute the seasonal index for each season -quarters for our example. The seasonal index for a specific season is the average for that specific season divided by the average of all the given data. For example, the seasonal index for January would be for the average for all January observations divided by the average for all data. For quarters, the seasonal index for the first quarter would be the average value of the first quarter data divided by the average of all data. Mathematically, we can pursue this as follows: there are n rows (a row for each quarter, and i is the row index), and there are m columns (a column for each year, and j is the column index). The value of quantity demand for the jth quarter for year i will be represented by D_{ij}, Seasonal indices (SI_{ij} are as follows:

$$SI_i = \frac{(\sum_{j=1}^{m} D_{ij})/m}{(\sum_{m=1}^{m} \sum_{i=1}^{n} D_{ij})/mn} \qquad \text{EQ 3-12}$$

Using this relationship, we can determine seasonal indices for our example problem the way it is presented in Table 3.5.

Qtr.	Period	Year 1 Dem.	Period	Year 2 Dem.	Period	Year 3 Dem	SI
1	1	85	5	93	9	96	0.96
2	2	118	6	130	10	133	1.34
3	3	83	7	89	11	95	0.94
4	4	69	8	74	12	75	0.76

TABLE 3- 5. SEASONAL INDICES FOR TIME SERIES DATA

3.4.2   De-Seasonalize Data

The seasonal indices display the relative contribution each season makes to the aggregate demand. You will see from our calculations that the second quarter is the "busy" quarter, compared to quarters 1, 3 and 4.

The next step is to "de-seasonalize" the data by taking each observation and dividing it by its appropriate seasonal index. The de-seasonalized data for the ith quarter for the jth year will be represented by DS_{ij}, and is calculated as follows:

$$DS_{ij} = \frac{D_{ij}}{SI_i} \qquad\qquad \text{Eq 3- 13}$$

The above formula filters out the seasonality and isolates any trend which may exist, and linear (or nonlinear) regression can be used to capture the trend. Figure 3.5. Note that the seasonality (repeating peaks and valleys) have been removed, showing only the presence of the trend.

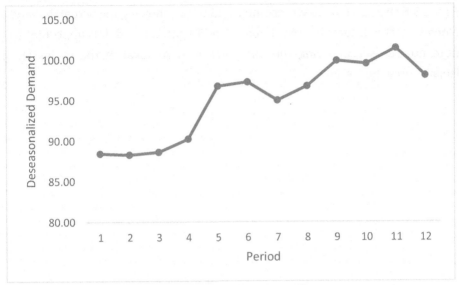

FIGURE 3- 5. DE-SEASONALIZED DATA

3.4.3 Capture Trend

To capture the trend, we simply fit a model where the de-seasonalized data is the dependent variable and the independent variable is the time period. Before showing this model, however, we need to convert our de-seasonalized data from DS_{ij} form to DS_i, form. We do this via the following:

$$t = nj + i, \forall i = 1, \dots n; \forall j = 0, \dots, m - 1 \qquad \text{EQ 3- 14}$$

Do not place too much concern with the above formula -the appropriate period numbers (t) are listed next to the actual demand values. We can fit the linear model to capture the trend exposed by our de-seasonalized data:

$$\widehat{DS}_t = a + bt \qquad \text{EQ 3- 15}$$

Fitting this model with our de-seasonalized data, we have captured the trend, with an intercept of 87.12 and a slope of 1.21, resulting in the following fit/forecast model:

$$F_t = 87.12 + 1.21t \qquad\qquad \text{EQ 3- 16}$$

Figure 3.6 shows what we've accomplished so far, showing the actual demand along with the deseasonalized demand and its fitted trend. It is important to note how de-seasonalizing the data results in removal of the cycles and isolates only the trend.

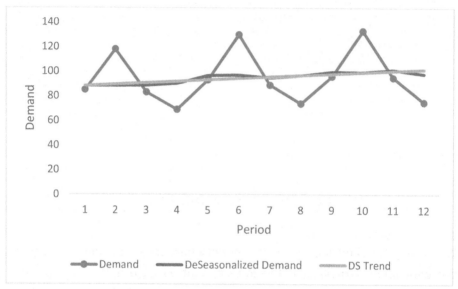

FIGURE 3- 6. FITTED DESEASONALIZED TREND

3.4.4   Fit and Forecast

The final step to this forecasting approach is to re-incorporate seasonality and then extrapolate our estimates into the future. First, let us perform back-forecasting to compare our estimates with the actual data. To do this, we simply multiply our trend by the appropriate seasonal index:

$$F_t = (87.12 + 1.21t)SI_i \qquad\qquad \text{EQ 3- 17}$$

Here, SI_t; is the appropriate seasonal index corresponding with period t. Simply put, multiplying the fitted trend by the appropriate seasonal index puts the seasonality "back in." We can then determine the MAD by comparing the back-forecasts to the given data:

$$MAD = \frac{1}{P}\sum_{t=1}^{P} |D_t - F_t|$$

EQ 3- 18

For our example, the MAD is 1.55. On average, our back-forecast is 1.55 units different from the actual.

At this point, to forecast, we only need to "extend" our line into the future by adding new values oft, and using the appropriate SI; values to re-seasonalize our data, along with our trend model. A comparison of our actual data and our fit/forecast data one year into the future is shown below. Notice how closely the fit/forecast line matches up with the actual values, which is suggestive of a good fit/forecast. Figure 3.7 illustrates this.

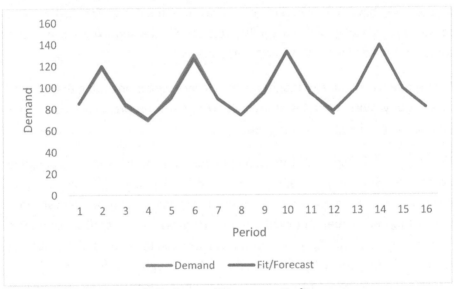

FIGURE 3- 7. ACTUAL DEMAND VS FIT/FORECAST

The notation in this section has been complicated due to the fact that we must change from double-subscripted notation ("ij") to time-series notation ("t"). Because of this complicating force, the Appendix is provided for a more deliberated pursuit of this example problem.

3.5 Parsimony

There is a very large arsenal of forecasting tools. In this chapter, we have covered some simple, yet very useful tools. There is always a temptation to increase the R^2 or decrease the MAD term a little bit so as to boast a better forecast. When forecasting, let us remember that we may have to explain the details of our forecasting approach to someone else - perhaps someone who is not quantitatively versed. Because of this, it is very important to keep our forecasts as straightforward as possible. Your objective should not be to impress the "impress" the client, but to "inform" the client.

Parsimony should always rule the day. ALWAYS.

3.6 Conclusions

Forecasting is a very powerful topic. Even though this book is introductory in nature, we have covered linear forecasting, nonlinear forecasting and seasonal forecasting. With just a little bit of practice and experience, these tools can provide immense value to organizations.

My experience in industry taught me that forecasting is one thing that is done quite poorly. With just a bit of practice from the tools presented here, poor forecasting can be greatly improved.

The "real-world" aspect of forecasting needs to be addressed via a personal experience. Several years ago, I was hired by a public utility company in northern Maine to provide revenue forecasts. I used a sophisticated forecasting technique, and excitedly reported my results to the client. The client was happy with the work, but then proceeded to tell me that we needed to "tweak" the forecasts based on things he thought would happen in the future - litigation related to pricing, availability of electricity, etc. Because of these real world issues with which I was unfamiliar, we increased our forecast 5% for one month, and decreased our forecast 3% for another month, etc. In other words, we adjusted the scientific forecasts to accommodate realistic issues. As the years have passed, this particular experience has become very salient to me. The forecasting we have covered in chapter has been a scientific pursuit, but the best forecasts should always consider real world issues that can occur.

3.7 Exercises

1.   The time series "SeriesG" documents domestic air travelers (in 1,000s) from January, 1959 to December, 1970. Find the most appropriate forecasting model and forecast domestic air travel for all months of 1971.

2.   The time series "SnowShovels" shows demand for snow shovels from January, 2006 through December, 2010. Find the most appropriate forecasting model, and forecast snow shovel demand for all months of 2011.

3.   The time series "TimeSeries1" shows Advertising dollars for a specific day, and the sales the following day. Using the most appropriate forecasting model, explain the relationship between Advertising dollars and the next day's sales.

4.   The time series "TimeSeries2" shows" monthly demand for a certain entity. Find the most appropriate forecasting model and forecast demand one year into the future.

5.   Jim Bob's Video Shoppe is interested in forecasting quarterly rentals from the data set ("JimBobs"). Use this data set to forecast one year into the future.

6.   A dentist's office bills on a bi-monthly basis. This means every two months. January/February is one billing period, March/April is the next billing period, etc. The "DentistBilling" data set details billing for the most recent three years: 2010, 2011 and 2012. Choose the most appropriate model and forecast one period into the future.

Appendix: Development of Seasonal Forecasting Problem

Consider the data shown in the forecasting chapter:

Quarter	t	D_t	t	D_t	t	D_t	Avg.	SI
1	1	85	5	93	9	96	91.33	0.96
2	2	118	6	130	10	133	127.00	1.34
3	3	83	7	89	11	95	89.00	0.94
4	4	69	8	74	12	75	72.67	0.76

TABLE 3. GIVEN DATA WITH SEASONAL INDICES SHOWN

This table is different in that instead of Demand in double subscripted notation, it is subscripted by time period, while the table's row's are organized by quarter. This easily lets us calculated the seasonal averages and seasonal indices, which are shown. The table is now re-organized so that all time periods are in a single column.

Period	SI_i	D_t	DS_t
1	0.96	85	88.41
2	1.31	118	88.27
3	0.94	83	88.60
4	0.76	69	90.21
5	0.96	93	96.73
6	1.31	130	97.24
7	0.94	89	95.00
8	0.76	74	96.74
9	0.96	96	99.85
10	1.31	133	99.49
11	0.94	95	101.40
12	0.76	75	98.05

TABLE 4. DATA IN COLUMN FORMAT WITH SEASONALIZED DEMAND

From the deseasonalized data, we capture the trend, having an intercept of 87.12 and a slope of 1.21. Applying these terms to the de-seasonalized data, we have the following fitted trend:

Period	SI_i	D_t	DS_t	Trend
1	0.96	85	88.41	88.34
2	1.31	118	88.27	89.55
3	0.94	83	88.60	90.76
4	0.76	69	90.21	91.97
5	0.96	93	96.73	93.18
6	1.31	130	97.24	94.39
7	0.94	89	95.00	95.61
8	0.76	74	96.74	96.82
9	0.96	96	99.85	98.03
10	1.31	133	99.49	99.24
11	0.94	95	101.40	100.45
12	0.76	75	98.05	101.66

TABLE 5. FITTED TREND

The final step in this process is to re-incorporate seasonality back into our model, and extend our fitted trend four periods (one year) into the future. This is shown below:

Period	SI_i	D_t	DS_t	Trend	Fit/Forecast
1	0.96	85	88.41	88.34	84.93
2	1.31	118	88.27	89.55	119.71
3	0.94	83	88.60	90.76	85.03
4	0.76	69	90.21	91.97	70.35
5	0.96	93	96.73	93.18	89.59
6	1.31	130	97.24	94.39	126.19
7	0.94	89	95.00	95.61	89.57
8	0.76	74	96.74	96.82	74.06
9	0.96	96	99.85	98.03	94.25
10	1.31	133	99.49	99.24	132.67
11	0.94	95	101.40	100.45	94.11
12	0.76	75	98.05	101.66	77.76
13	0.96				98.90
14	1.31				139.15
15	0.94				98.65
16	0.76				81.47

TABLE 6. FITS AND FORECASTS

4. Decision Tree Analysis

Life is filled with decision-making. Some decisions are easy, some are difficult. In this chapter, we deal with the difficult decisions – at least from a quantitative standpoint. An example of an easy decision is one where we are offered two jobs – we will call them A and B. If jobs A and B are identical in every aspect, with the exception of compensation, we take the job offering the highest compensation. This decision is trivial.

Let's take this example one step further. Job A offers more compensation than does Job B, but Job B looks more promising in terms of professional growth. What is the likelihood for growth regarding Job B? How much growth is associated with Job B? All of a sudden this decision becomes less trivial because of the uncertainty associated with future professional growth opportunities. In short, we are confronted with a difficult decision.

In this chapter, we explore the tools used to analyze decisions that involved uncertainty.

4.1 Decision Trees

To address these decisions involving uncertainty, we first itemize the list of options and call them **alternatives**. We will assume there are n unique alternatives, and refer to alternative i as a_i. Each alternative has an uncertain **outcome** that does not present itself until after the decision is made. We will assume that there are m possible outcomes for each alternative. Each outcome has a certain probability of occurring. We will refer to the probability of outcome j occurring as p_j. Each outcome has an associated **payoff**. We will refer to the payoff associated with alternative i and outcome j as P_{ij}.

We combine all of this information via a decision tree – a graphical representation of all alternatives and associated outcomes and payoffs. A rectangular node represents where a decision needs to be made. A round node represents an outcome of which we are uncertain. Each outcome has some probability of occurring. After the uncertainty is represented, we are shown the payoff in monetary or similar units.

As an example, consider the decision of whether or not to bring an umbrella to work in the morning. There are two alternatives: bring an umbrella or do not bring an umbrella. For each alternative, there is uncertainty: rain or no rain. Our decision is influenced by the possible outcomes. This problem is represented by the decision tree shown in Figure 4.1

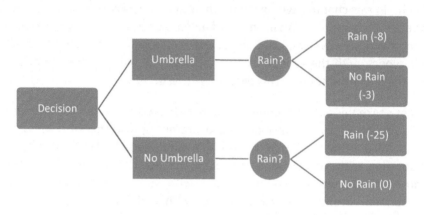

FIGURE 4.1. DECISION TREE FOR UMBRELLA PROBLEM

There are four outcomes for this problem: (1) we bring an umbrella and it rains; (2) we bring an umbrella and it does not rain; (3) we do not bring an umbrella and it rains; and (4) we do not bring an umbrella and it rains. The payoffs associated with these outcomes are: -8, -3 -25 and 0. These payoffs are in units of **utility** – a non-monetary unit associated with success. "Utility" is often used in economics.

4.2 Decision Strategies

We are not unable to make a decision (choose an alternative) until we know what it is we wish to accomplish. As such, prior to making a decision, we need to pursue a particular strategy. In decision analysis, there are several strategies, but we will cover the three most basic here.

4.2.1 Optimistic Strategy ("Maximax")

If we are optimistic, we assume the best will happen. In this case, we choose our alternative assuming the best possible outcome will occur. This means that for each alternative, we select the most favorable outcome and then select the alternative with the best overall outcome. For our umbrella problem, then, we choose accordingly:

$$Max[max(-8, -3), max(-25, 0)] \qquad \text{EQ 4-1}$$

This simplifies to the following:

$$Max[-3, 0] = 0 \qquad \text{EQ 4-2}$$

This **"maximax"** value of 0 is the payoff associated with not bringing an umbrella, because we assume there will be no rain. The upshot of this is that under the optimistic strategy, we choose not to bring an umbrella because we don't think it is going to rain.

4.2.2   Pessimistic Strategy ("Maximin")

If we are pessimistic, we assume the worst will happen, and the make the best decision accordingly. This means that for each alternative, we assume the worst will happen, and then choose the alternative that provides us with the best result. For our umbrella problem, we proceed as follows:

$$Max[min(-8, -3), min(-25, 0)] \qquad \text{EQ 4-3}$$

This simplifies to the following:

$$Max[-8, -25] = -8 \qquad \text{EQ 4-4}$$

The **"maximin"** value here is -8, the payoff associated with bringing an umbrella when it rains. This means that the best pessimistic decision is to bring an umbrella because we think it will rain.

4.2.3   Expected Value Strategy

The first two strategies covered are important strategies, but for this example, the results are self-obviating – the optimist will not bring an umbrella because they do not think it will rain, while the pessimist will bring an umbrella because they think it will rain.

We will now examine another strategy that is more rooted in mathematics and specifically probability. We will explore the expected value strategy, which is based on what we expect each alternative's value to be. The expected value for alternative a_i is represented as $E(a_i)$ and is determined as follows:

$$E(a_i) = \sum_{j=1}^{m} p_j P_{ij}$$

EQ 4-5

For our umbrella problem, we will assume a probability of rain to be 0.25, which implies a probability of no rain as 0.75.

For the umbrella alternative, our expected value is:

$$(.25)(-8) + (.75)(-3) = -4.25$$

EQ 4-6

For the no umbrella alternative, our expected value is:

$$(.25)(-25) + (.75)(0) = -6.25$$

EQ 4-7

Comparing the expected values of the two alternatives, we wish to maximize:

$$\text{Max}[-4.25, -6.25] = -4.25$$

EQ 4-8

Our best alternative has an expected value of -4.25, and is associated with the "bring umbrella alternative." As such, using expected value, we should not bring the umbrella. We will call this value of -4.25 as the **expected value**.

4.3 Expected Value of Perfect Information

We can take our discussion of expected value one step further. When we calculated our expected value (EV) above, we essentially calculated the **expected value under uncertainty** because we were not certain what would happen in the future. Let's assume for a moment that we have the ability to make our decision with advanced knowledge of what will happen. For example, if we knew in advance it was going to rain, we would bring our umbrella, and if we knew in advance it was not going to rain, we would not bring our umbrella. In terms of the mathematical approach to this problem, the **expected value under certainty** would be as follows:

$$EVUC = \sum_{j=1}^{m} p_j \cdot \max_i(P_{ij})$$

EQ 4-9

For our umbrella problem, assume we have advance knowledge that it will rain. With that knowledge, we select an umbrella as that payoff is better than the payoff associated with not bringing un umbrella when it rains (max[-8, -

25] = -8). With advance knowledge that it will not rain, we would choose not to bring an umbrella because of the higher payoff (max[-3, 0] = 0). Because our advance knowledge of rain will occur 25% of the time, and advance knowledge of no rain will occur 75% of the time, our expected value under certainty value is as follows:

$$EVUC = (-8)(.25) + (0)(.75) = -2 \qquad \text{Eq 4-10}$$

In other words, under certainty – with advance knowledge of what will happen, we expect a payoff of -2.

To summarize, under uncertainty, we have an expected value of -4.25. We refer to this value as the expected value, or the **expected value under uncertainty** (EVUU). Under certainty, we have an expected value of -2. We call this the expected value under certainty (EVUC). The difference between these two values is referred to as the expected value with perfect information (EVPI). Mathematically, this value is as follows:

$$EVPI = EVUC - EVUU \qquad \text{Eq 4-11}$$

For our example, the EVPI is -2 - (-4.25) = 2.25. This value is always positive, and numerically represents the difference between being certain and being uncertain. Another way to interpret this is maximum amount you should "pay" to eliminate uncertainty.

4.4 An Example

Let is consider a monetary example with three investment alternatives: Bonds, Stocks and CDs. Each alternative has three possible outcomes: growth, stagnation and inflation. We assume that the probability of growth is 50%, the probability of stagnation is 30%, and the probability of inflation is 20%. Figure 4.2 shows the details of this problem, including payoffs in decision tree format.

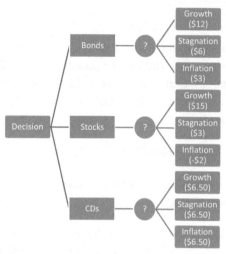

FIGURE 4 2. DECISION TREE FOR INVESTMENT PROBLEM

Table 4.1 displays this data in table format for easy calculations.

Alternative	Outcomes			Results		
	Growth (p = 0.5)	Stag. (p = 0.3)	Inflation (p = 0.2)	Max	Min	EVUU
Bonds	$12	$6	$3	$12	$3	$8.4
Stocks	$15	$3	-$2	$15	-$2	$8
CDs	$6.5	$6.5	$6.5	$6.5	$6.5	$6.5
Max Val.	$15	$6.5	$6.5	$15	$6.5	$8.4
Decision	N/A			Stocks	CDs	Bonds

TABLE 4 1. DETAILS OF MONETARY EXAMPLE DECISION TREE PROBLEM

For each alternative, the maximum, minimum and expected value payoffs have been determined. The optimist would choose Stocks because $15, the best possible outcome would occur via the Stocks decision. The pessimist would choose CDs, because $6.5 is the best outcome assuming the worst will happen. When pursuing expected value, Bonds is the best decision, because they provide the highest expected value ($8.4).

The expected value under certainty is as follows:

$$EVUC = 15(0.5) + 6.5(0.3) + 6.5(0.3) = 10.75 \qquad \text{EQ 4-12}$$

Now that we understand the expected value under uncertainty is $8.4 and the expected value under certainty is $10.75, we can calculate the expected value of perfect information as ($10.75 − $8.4 = $2.35). To put this result into a monetary context, we can say that the value of eliminating uncertainty is $2.35 – if we hired someone with the ability to somehow remove uncertainty from our problem, we should pay them no more than $2.35 for their services.

4.5 Conclusions

Decision analysis is an important topic in that it bridges the theoretical and applied worlds. I have personally never constructed a decision tree for a decision that I have needed to make. Nevertheless, a decision tree does structure a decision in terms of options, associated uncertainties and their interrelationships, which is important.

Another thing worth considering is that our payoffs are subjected to interpretation. In our umbrella example, we talk about how being in the rain without an umbrella is somehow a "bad" thing. That is basically stated from the perspective of someone traveling to work or classes at the university. Imagine, however, a nervous farmer in South Dakota worried about a dried-out corn crop in August. If that farmer is caught in a downpour without an umbrella will they be upset? Of course not – they will be relieved and happy. This point needs to be made because payoffs need to be valued from the proper perspective.

Another issue to consider is the concept of outcomes. In our example problems, our outcomes are "discrete" – either a specific outcome occurs or does not occur. In reality that is not the case. For our example problem, we have outcomes that state it is either raining or it is not raining. Unfortunately, there are times, especially in places like Seattle, San Francisco or London where we are in a fog, and we're not sure if it is raining or not – such situations are not discrete. The thinking behind quantification of payoffs and outcomes is part of a larger social science known as decision/utility theory.

Finally, it is worth mentioning the concept of expected value with perfect information. As we define this concept, we describe it as the value of eliminating uncertainty. In reality, of course, we cannot eliminate uncertainty. If we had that ability, there is essentially no reason in having this book. Nevertheless, we do perform better as organizations and individuals if we can minimize uncertainty. Consider financial service companies like ETrade and TDAmeritrade. These corporations, along with others, boast of research they provide which "reduces" uncertainty, and subsequently improving portfolio performance. They are essentially claiming that they have the ability to reduce uncertainty. Regardless of whether or not these vague claims are true, they do entice the investor to consider the value of the advertised research – the claim of reduced uncertainty, which lies at the heart of decision analysis.

4.6 Exercises

For these questions, address the following: state what the optimist would do; state what the pessimist would do; state what one would do using expected value as a strategy; and state the expected value of perfect information.

1. I have some money to invest, and I have three investment options: ChemicalBrothers, MötleyCrüe, and ConcreteBlonde. ChemicalBrothers has a payoff of $10 when a good market occurs, and a loss of $5 when a bad market occurs. MötleyCrüe has a payoff of $7 when a good market occurs, and a loss of $4 when a bad market occurs. ConcreteBlonde has a payoff of $5 when a good market occurs, and a loss of $2 when a bad market occurs. A good market has a 40% chance of occurring.

2. You have been given some money to invest, and you are considering three different options for your investment choice: AlphaStuds, BetaStuds and GammaStuds. Under a favorable market, AlphaStuds will return $100, but lose $30 under an unfavorable market. Under a favorable market, BetaStuds will return $75, but lose $25 under an unfavorable market. GammaStuds will return $60 under a favorable market, but lose $15 under an unfavorable market. A favorable market has a 60% of occurring, while an unfavorable market has a 40% chance of occurring. All money must be invested in one of the three options – distributing the investment among multiple investments is not permitted.

3. I have some money to invest. I will invest all of it in either RustStuds or JetElectro. RustStuds will return a gain of $10 in a favorable market and a loss of $3 in an unfavorable market. JetElectro will return a gain $14 in a favorable market, and a loss of $5 in an unfavorable market. The probability of the market being favorable is 60%, while there is a 40% probability of an unfavorable market.

4. I have some money to invest, and I'm considering three possible investments: AcmeCorp, BestCorp, and CoolioCorp. When the return is favorable, I can expect a $1,000 payoff from AcmeCorp, a $500 return from BestCorp, and a $400 return from CoolioCorp. When the return is unfavorable, I can expect a loss of $300 from AcmeCorp, a loss of $200 from BestCorp, and a loss of $100 from CoolioCorp. There is a 55% probability of a favorable return and a 45% probability of an unfavorable return.

5. I have $1M to invest. I have narrowed my investment choices down to two possible alternatives: AlphaTron and OmegaTron. I must invest all of the $1M in one of the securities – mixing the investment between the two securities is not permitted. Under good market conditions, AlphaTron will provide a return of $100K, while OmegaTron will provide a return of $60K. Under average market conditions, AlphaTron will provide a return of $20K, while OmegaTron will provide a return of $10K. Under bad market conditions, AlphaTron will lose $60K, while OmegaTron will lose $30K. Good market conditions are estimated to occur with a 40% probability, average and bad market conditions are each estimated to occur with a 30% probability.

5. Mathematical Programming

Up to this point, we have essentially covered data analysis. That is, we've been given data, we study the data, then we attempt to put the data in perspective – we would like to say something interesting about the data. We take a completely different tack in this, our final chapter.

Here, we are given some basic information, such as unit profit or unit cost for specific entities, a set of rules to follow, and aggregate this information such that some objective is optimized, such as maximization of profit or minimization of cost.

The process of doing this is called mathematical programming, and it requires us to build a model to optimize. This process is radically different from everything else covered to this point.

5.1 Introduction

To illustrate how mathematical programming works, we will start with a simple example. Consider a furniture company that makes two different types of chairs: Model A and Model B. Each unit of Model A results in a profit of $7/chair, while each unit of Model B results in a profit of $5/chair. When each unit of Model A is made, two assembly hours are required, and six finishing hours are required. When each unit of Model B is made, one assembly hour is required, and seven finishing hours are required. Each week, 1,600 assembly hours are available, and 8,400 finishing hours are available.

The relevant question then becomes how many units of Model A and Model B should be made such that the company's total weekly profit is maximized?

5.2 Linear Programming

The problem above has a few salient features that are noteworthy. First of all, there is a clearly-defined objective (maximize total profit). Secondly, there are entities in which the user has some control (the number of units of Models A and B to make). Finally, there are rules requiring adherence (limited assembly and finishing capacity).

These three salient features present themselves in mathematical programming problems. We must take this information and convert it into a mathematical model. This process is called **formulation**. When formulating a mathematical programming problem, we first take the entities over which we control and convert them into **decision variables**. These decision variables quantify the entities we control. For this example, we state our decision variables as follows:

x_A = the number of units of Model A to produce
x_B = the number of units of Model B to produce

Next, we consider the our objective to maximize our total profit, bearing in mind that we make $7 for each unit of Model A, and $5 for each unit of Model B. Combining the unit profits with the associated decision variables, we have the **objective function**, which in this case is to be maximized:

$$\text{Max: } 7x_A + 5x_B \qquad \qquad \text{EQ 5-1}$$

The last major hurdle of our effort involves converting the rules we must obey into mathematical form. For assembly, we must realize that each unit of Model A requires two hours of assembly labor, and each unit of Model B requires one hour of assembly labor, and we are limited to 1,600 total assembly hours in a one-week period. From a mathematical perspective we construct a **constraint**, and it is as follows:

$$2x_A + 1x_B \leq 1,600 \text{ (Assembly Hours)} \qquad \qquad \text{EQ 5-2}$$

Using similar logic for the finishing constraint, we realize that each unit of Model A requires six hours of finishing, and each unit of Model B requires seven hours of finishing, and we have 8,400 finishing hours available for our one-week period, we can construct the following finishing constraint:

$$6x_A + 7x_B \leq 8,400 \text{ (Finishing Hours)} \qquad \qquad \text{EQ 5-3}$$

Finally, we must state that our decision variables are not permitted to take on negative values. These non-negativity constraints are stated as follows:

$$x_A, x_B \geq 0 \text{ (Non-Negativity Constraints)} \qquad \qquad \text{EQ 5-4}$$

We have now formulated the problem at hand. Typically, we present the entire formulation in concise format as follows:

$$\text{Max: } 7x_A + 5x_B$$
$$\text{Subject to:}$$
$$2x_A + 1x_B \leq 1{,}600 \text{ (Assembly Hours)}$$
$$6x_A + 7x_B \leq 8{,}400 \text{ (Finishing Hours)}$$
$$x_A, x_B \geq 0 \text{ (Non-Negativity Constraints)}$$

EQ 5-5

The words "Subject to" always imply a subsequent set of "rules" that must be followed.

The above is a formulation of a Linear Programming problem. The word "linear" is included because the objective function and all constraints are in linear form. This is not always the case, but it is the most basic and understandable form of mathematical programming.

At this point, we have formulated our problem, but we have yet to make any progress regarding our optimal, or "best" solution.

5.3 Solver

Solving mathematical programming problems is an entire field within itself, and is far beyond the scope of this book. This field is typically referred to as "Operations Research" or "Management Science," and these fields are very mathematically intense. Fortunately, Microsoft Excel can be used to solve the most basic types of problems. Specifically, there is a built-in Excel tool called "Solver" that can assist in finding the optimal solution.

Before invoking Solver, the problem must be put into Excel is spreadsheet form. There are countless ways to do this, but some sort of structured effort simplifies the process. Figure 5-1 details how our example problem was inputted into Excel.

	A	B	C	D	E	F
1		Model A	Model B		Total	
2	Quantity	0	0		$ -	
3	Unit Profit	$ 7	$ 5			
4					LHS	RHS
5	Assembly	2	1		0	1,600
6	Finishing	6	7		0	8,400
7						
8	E2: =SUMPRODUCT(B3:C3,B2:C2)					
9	E5: =SUMPRODUCT(B5:C5,B2:C2)					
10	E6: =SUMPRODUCT(B6:C6,B2:C2)					

FIGURE 5-1. EXCEL FORMULATION FOR EXAMPLE PROBLEM

The spreadsheet organizes Model A and Model B data into separate columns, while decision variable values ("Quantity"), unit profit values, assembly and finishing constraint data are detailed in rows. Coefficients are inputted in the corresponding cells. It is good practice to color-code decision variable cells and the objective function cell. For this example, decision variables are coded yellow, while the objective function value is teal. There are three cells which display calculated results: E2 for the total profit; E5 for the assembly hours consumed; and E6 for the finishing hours consumed. These formulae details are displayed above – they are the Excel version of the objective function and the left-hand side (LHS) of the two constraints. The right hand side (RHS) constraint values are shown in the appropriate cells. Such is the formulation of the problem at hand.

To actually "solve" the problem, we invoke Solver via the "Data" menu option. The Solver box displays, and we are ready to tell Solver our problem details. Figure 5-2. shows the Solver box, with all required input provided.

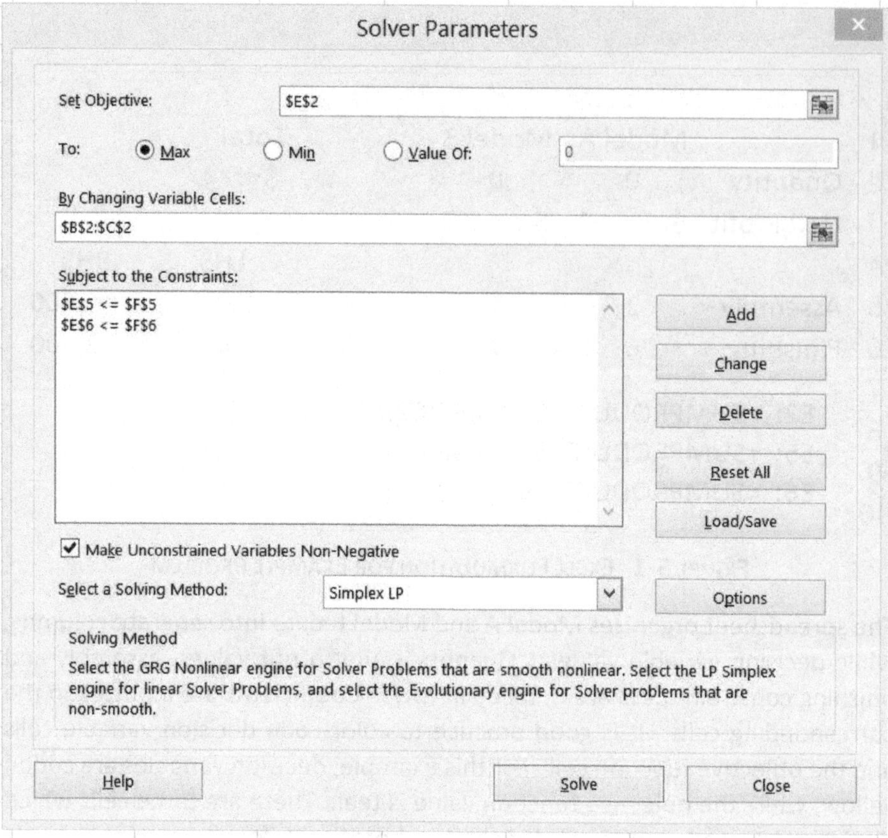

FIGURE 5-2. SOLVER FOR EXAMPLE PROBLEM

To provide Solver with the required information, we first need to tell Solver which cell contains the objective function value. In our case it is E2 (the teal cell in our example). Next we need to let Solver know which type of objective we have. In our case, we wish to maximize our objective function, so we select "Max." Next, we need to tell Solver about our decision variables. As such, when prompted with "By Changing Variable Cells," we simply select the range of cells that are decision variables (the yellow cells in our example). Next we need to add our constraints. In order to do that, we click the "Add" button in the "Subject to the Constraints" section. When we do this, we see a new box appear, similar to the one shown in Figure 5-3.

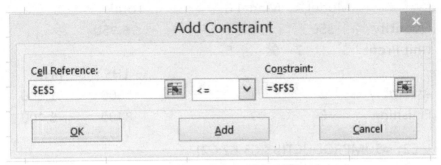

FIGURE 5-3. ADDING A CONSTRAINT

To complete this box, we enter the left-hand-side (LHS) value in the box for "Cell Reference" and the right-hand-side (RHS) value in the box for "Constraint." The "type" of constraint must also be selected from the drop-down box – for our example, we have a "≤" type. Figure 13.3 shows details for our "Assembly Labor" constraint. When finished, we click "Add" so that we can proceed similarly for the "Finishing Labor" constraint. When finished with that, we click the OK button, which will return us to the Solver form shown in Figure 5-2.

Next, the box should be checked when asked "Make Unconstrained Variables Non-Negative." This ensures that our decision variables will not be permitted to assume negative values (non-negativity constraints). Finally, the Solving Method should be "Simplex LP." This choice uses the traditional method for solving linear programming problems.

At this point, the "Solve" button should be clicked. After receiving a message stating that Solver was successful in finding an optimal solution, the spreadsheet will display the optimal solution. Figure 5-4 shows what we have for our example problem.

	A	B	C	D	E	F
1		Model A	Model B		Total	
2	Quantity	350	900		$6,950	
3	Unit Profit	$ 7	$ 5			
4					LHS	RHS
5	Assembly	2	1		1600	1,600
6	Finishing	6	7		8400	8,400
7						
8	E2: =SUMPRODUCT(B3:C3,B2:C2)					
9	E5: =SUMPRODUCT(B5:C5,B2:C2)					
10	E6: =SUMPRODUCT(B6:C6,B2:C2)					

FIGURE 5-4. OPTIMIZED SOLUTION FOR EXAMPLE PROBLEM

From inspection of Figure 5-4, we see that our optimal solution. We are told that 350 units of Model A and 900 units of Model B provide us our maximized total profit of $6,950. As we examine our constraints, we see that our constraints have not been violated – we have used all of our available assembly hours and finishing hours.

Solver gives us the ability to solve mathematical programming problems in Excel. Experience has suggested that converting a problem from a mathematical formulation to Excel formulation does take some practice. From this point forward, Solver will not be detailed in example problems. Instead, only mathematical formulations will be shown. Nevertheless, all mathematical programming problems covered in this chapter are available with the data sets.

5.4 Other Linear Programming Problem Types

The example problem above is probably the most basic type of linear programming problem. There are, however, many general types of linear programming problems, that run the gamut from trivial to quite complex. This section will detail a few of the most common types of linear programming problems.

5.4.1   Assignment Problem

Consider a problem where we need to assign four different factory workers to four different jobs. Each worker has some varying degree of skill at each specific job. For convenience, we will use an hourly cost to quantify a worker's skill level for a specific job – the higher the worker's skill level, the lower the hourly cost. The overall objective is to assign the four workers to the four jobs such that the total hourly cost is minimized. Consider the following cost table:

Worker\Job	Assembly	Delivery	Repair	Welding
Al	18	5	14	16
Billy	12	9	7	14
Chris	10	16	6	8
Dave	14	12	18	9

TABLE 5-1. COST TABLE FOR ASSIGNMENT PROBLEM

For example, if Chris were assigned to the welding job, $8/hour would be contributed to the total cost.

The mathematical formulation for this problem is reasonably straightforward. First, the decision variables are assigned in a tabular fashion via the following:

$$x_{ij} = 1 \text{ if worker i assigned to job j; 0 otherwise} \qquad \text{EQ 5-6}$$

As this point, the binary nature of the decision variables should not be worrisome – this is addressed shortly. The objective function then multiplies the decision variables with their corresponding coefficients. Mathematically, this is as follows:

$$\text{Min: } 18x_{11} + 5x_{12} + 14x_{13} + \ldots + 9x_{44} \qquad \text{EQ 5-7}$$

Because each worker must be assigned to exactly one job, we have the following constraints:

$$\text{Subject to:}$$
$$x_{11} + x_{12} + x_{13} + x_{14} = 1 \text{ (Al)} \qquad \text{EQ 5-8}$$
$$x_{21} + x_{22} + x_{23} + x_{24} = 1 \text{ (Billy)}$$
$$x_{31} + x_{32} + x_{33} + x_{34} = 1 \text{ (Chris)}$$

$$x_{41} + x_{42} + x_{43} + x_{44} = 1 \text{ (Dave)}$$

Likewise, each job must be assigned exactly one worker. Mathematically, we can state this as follows:

$$x_{11} + x_{21} + x_{31} + x_{41} = 1 \text{ (Assembly)}$$
$$x_{12} + x_{22} + x_{32} + x_{42} = 1 \text{ (Delivery)}$$
$$x_{13} + x_{23} + x_{33} + x_{43} = 1 \text{ (Repair)}$$
$$x_{14} + x_{24} + x_{34} + x_{44} = 1 \text{ (Welding)}$$

EQ 5-9

An optimal solution to this problem is to assignment Al to Delivery, Bill to Repair, Chris to Assembly, and Dave to Welding, for a total hourly cost of $5 + +$7 + $10 + $9 = $31. These costs associated with these assignments are italicized in the cost table above. We are not prepared to say that this is the optimal solution, we can only say this is an optimal solution. There could be multiple solutions resulting in a minimized cost of $31, but we are certain that $31 is in fact the minimized cost.

A comment above was made about the "binary" nature of the decision variables. The decision variables end up being binary – that is, they take on values of 0 or 1 because the constraints all sum to one, forcing a single value of "1" in each row and column. Further discussion of these specific mathematics is left for a more comprehensive course.

It should be noted that this formulation can be generalized into a more compact form, shows as follows:

$$Min: \sum_{i=1}^{n} \sum_{j=1}^{n} c_{ij} x_{ij}$$

Subject to:

$$\sum_{j=1}^{n} x_{ij} = 1, \forall i,$$

EQ 5-10

$$\sum_{i=1}^{n} x_{ij} = 1, \forall j$$

The c_{ij} values are simply the cost coefficients associated with assigning worker i to job j. The first set of constraints force each worker to be assigned to a single job, while the second set of constraints force each job to have one worker.

5.4.2 Transportation Problem

Another important linear programming problem is the Transportation Problem. Here, we are given some number (n) of supply sources that must ship products to some number (m) of destinations at minimal cost. The supply sources have limited capacity, and the destinations have a demand that must be met.

Table 5-2 details a Transportation Problem, with four sources and five destinations. The demand (in units) for each destination appears in the bottom row. The per-unit shipping costs are provided in the top four rows. For example, it costs $20 to ship one unit from Greensboro to Duck. Each source has a capacity of supplying 1,800 units. We wish to ship such that demand is met for all destinations without exceeding supply at a minimal cost.

Source \ Destination	Asheville	Duck	Durham	Gastonia	Raleigh
Winston-Salem	10	25	8	7	9
Charlotte	12	26	9	3	11
Greensboro	13	20	7	8	8
High Point	14	21	6	9	7
Demand	800	300	1,000	900	2,000

TABLE 5-2. COST AND DEMAND DETAIL FOR TRANSPORTATION.

The formulation for this problem shares some similarities with that of the Assignment Problem. First we define our decision variables:

$$x_{ij} = \text{units shipped from source i to destination j} \qquad \text{EQ 5-11}$$

This provides us with the following objective function:

$$\text{Min: } 10x_{12} + 25x_{12} + \dots + 7x_{45} \qquad \text{EQ 5-12}$$

In order for the supply not be exceeded for each source, we must provide the following constraints:

$$\text{Subject to:} \qquad \text{EQ 5-13}$$
$$x_{11} + x_{12} + x_{13} + x_{14} + x_{15} \le 1,800 \text{ (Winston-Salem)}$$

$$x_{21} + x_{22} + x_{23} + x_{24} + x_{25} \leq 1,800 \text{ (Charlotte)}$$
$$x_{31} + x_{32} + x_{33} + x_{34} + x_{35} \leq 1,800 \text{ (Greensboro)}$$
$$x_{41} + x_{42} + x_{43} + x_{44} + x_{45} \leq 1,800 \text{ (High Point)}$$

The demand constraints are as follows:

$$x_{11} + x_{21} + x_{31} + x_{41} = 800 \text{ (Asheville)}$$
$$x_{12} + x_{22} + x_{32} + x_{42} = 300 \text{ (Duck)}$$
$$x_{13} + x_{23} + x_{33} + x_{43} = 1,000 \text{ (Durham)} \qquad \text{EQ 5-14}$$
$$x_{14} + x_{24} + x_{34} + x_{44} = 900 \text{ (Gastonia)}$$
$$x_{15} + x_{25} + x_{35} + x_{45} = 2,000 \text{ (Raleigh)}$$

Table 5-3 shows the optimal distribution from the sources to the destinations. The minimized cost is $37,900

Source \ Destination	Asheville	Duck	Durham	Gastonia	Raleigh
Winston-Salem	800	0	0	0	0
Charlotte	0	0	0	900	0
Greensboro	0	300	0	0	1,200
High Point	0	0	1,000	0	800

TABLE 5-3. OPTIMAL DISTRIBUTION FOR TRANSPORTATION PROBLEM

As is the case with the Assignment Problem, the Transportation Problem can also be generalized into the following form:

$$Min: \sum_{i=1}^{n} \sum_{j=1}^{m} c_{ij} x_{ij}$$

Subject to:

$$\sum_{j=1}^{m} x_{ij} \leq Supply_i, \forall i, \qquad \text{EQ 5-15}$$

$$\sum_{i=1}^{n} x_{ij} = Demand_j, \forall j$$

5.4.3   Blending Problem

The last type of linear programming problem discussed is the blending problem. The blending problem is where there is a need to combine ingredients into some finished product in a minimal cost or maximal profit fashion. These problems are typically more challenging to formulate than the ones previously discussed.

As an example, consider a company that combines two different components into three different animal feeds. The first component is a protein source, while the second is a carbohydrate source. Feed 1 must be at least 25% protein, and sells for $1.45/pound. Feed 2 must be at least 40% protein, and sells for $1.52/pound. Feed 3 must be at least 55% protein and sells for $1.60/pound. Component 1 costs $1.05/pound and the weekly supply is limited to 5,000 pounds. Component 2 costs $0.25/pound and the weekly supply is limited to 6,500 pounds. Demand for each of the three feeds is assumed to be unlimited. Our job is to mix the component for each of the three feeds such that the company's total profit is maximized.

This problem is more difficult to formulate as compared to the others covered. There are several ways to proceed, but the approach chosen here is believed to be the least complex. Let us first realize that there are two inputs (Protein and Carbohydrate sources) and three outputs (Feeds A, B and C). A decision variable will be defined for each input/output combination. As such, our decision variables are defined as follows:

$$x_{ij} = \text{pounds of component i used for feed j} \qquad \text{EQ 5-16}$$

Specific decision variable names and other relevant problem data are organized in Table 5-4.

	Feed A	Feed B	Feed C	Supply	Unit Cost
Comp. 1 (Protein)	x_{1A}	x_{1B}	x_{1C}	5,000	$1.05
Comp. 2 (Carb.)	x_{2A}	x_{2B}	x_{2C}	6,500	$0.25
Protein Minimum	25%	40%	55%		
Unit Profit	$1.45	$1.52	$1.60		

TABLE 5-4. DATA FOR BLENDING PROBLEM

To formulate the objective function, it must be realized that in order to maximize profit, we must maximize the difference between revenue and cost. In the context of this problem, the objective function is as follows:

$$\text{Max: } [1.45(x_{1A} + x_{2A}) + 1.52(x_{1B} + x_{2B}) + 1.60(x_{1C} + x_{2C})] \quad \text{EQ 5-17}$$
$$- [1.05(x_{1A} + x_{1B} + x_{1C}) + 0.25(x_{2A} + x_{2B} + x_{2C})]$$

The first part of the objective function is revenue, while the second part is cost. The supply constraints are more straightforward:

$$\text{Subject to:}$$
$$x_{1A} + x_{1B} + x_{1C} \leq 5,000 \text{ (Protein Component)} \quad \text{EQ 5-18}$$
$$x_{2A} + x_{2B} + x_{2C} \leq 6,500 \text{ (Carb. Component)}$$

The protein constraints can be constructed by relating the actual ratio of protein weight to total weight for each feed. This is done as follows:

$$x_{1A}/(x_{1A} + x_{2A}) \geq 0.25$$
$$x_{1B}/(x_{1B} + x_{2B}) \geq 0.40 \quad \text{EQ 5-19}$$
$$x_{1C}/(x_{1C} + x_{2C}) \geq 0.55$$

There is, however, a problem with these three constraints. They are nonlinear – there are decision variables in the numerator, which complicates the solution process. With some algebraic manipulation, however, they can be restored to linear form. When both sides of the constraints are multiplied by the denominator on the left-hand side, linear form is restored:

$$x_{1A} \geq 0.25(x_{1A} + x_{2A})$$
$$x_{1B} \geq 0.40(x_{1B} + x_{2B}) \quad \text{EQ 5-20}$$
$$x_{1C} \geq 0.55(x_{1C} + x_{2C})$$

The problem is now formulated, and Solver provides the following result with a maximized profit of $10,862.50.

	Feed A	Feed B	Feed C
Comp. 1 (Protein)	1104.17	0	3895.83
Comp. 2 (Carb.)	3312.50	0	3187.50

TABLE 5 5. OPTIMAL SOLUTION TO THE BLENDING PROBLEM

Solver determined that Feed B should not be made.

5.5 Integer Programming

When solving mathematical programming problems, there are times when it is necessary to guarantee our decision variables take on integer values. The example above shows a solution with non-integer decision variable values. Perhaps it is only possible to buy in one-pound units. As such, we would need to ensure our decision variables take on integer values.

Another relevant scenario is when we would like our optimal solution to decide whether or not a certain condition applies in our optimal solution. In other words, we would like to have the ability to impose certain logical scenarios in our effort to find an optimal solution.

Both of these scenarios can be addressed by a mathematical programming concept referred to as integer programming. The first type of integer programming is where we mandate certain decision variables to take on integer values, such as 0, 1, 2, ..., whereas the second scenario mandates that certain decision variables take on binary values – that is, values that are either 0 or 1. This second scenario might sound trivial on the surface, but binary variable add great power and flexibility to mathematical programming models.

5.5.1   Integer Decision Variables

As can be seen in Table 5-5, our optimal solution for the blending problem yields a non-integer solution. If it is not possible to purchase the components in partial pounds, it would be in our best interest to optimize when our decision variables are restricted to integer values. In Excel/Solver, this is straightforward to do. We need to add a constraint to classify all decision variables to take on integer values. This is illustrated in Figure 5-5.

	A	B	C	D	E	F	G
1	Component	Feed A	Feed B	Feed C	Sum	Supply	Unit Cost
2	1	1104.166667	0	3895.833	5000	5000	$ 1.05
3	2	3312.5	0	3187.5	6500	6500	$ 0.25
4							
5			Add Constraint				✕
6							
7		Cell Reference:			Constraint:		
8		$B$2:$D$3		int ∨	integer		
9	Uni						
10		OK		Add		Cancel	
11	Re						
12	Cost	$ 6,875.00					
13							
14	Profit	$ 10,862.50					
15							

FIGURE 5-5. STATING INTEGER VARIABLES FOR BLENDING PROBLEM

In the Constraints section, we click "Add." We then select the decision variables we wish to restrict as integer, and then select "int" in the drop-down box. We then click "OK" and then choose "Solve." Our new optimal solution is shown in Table 5-6.

	Feed A	Feed B	Feed C
Comp. 1 (Protein)	1104	2	3894
Comp. 2 (Carb.)	3311	3	3186

TABLE 5-6. OPTIMAL SOLUTION TO THE BLENDING PROBLEM

One should note that enforcing decision variables to take on integer values is not necessarily a matter of "rounding" variables accordingly. Decision variables can change to some significant degree. It is also worth noting that our maximized profit is now $10,862.35 – a small decrease from the earlier solution. Given that constraints have been added to this problem, we can only expect the optimized objective function value to worsen.

5.5.2   Binary Variables

The other salient feature in using integer variables is when we restrict decision variables to take on one of two possible values: zero or one. Such variables are called "binary" variables.[5] The use of binary variables enables us

---

[5] In Computer Science, these variables are referred to as "Boolean Variables."

to induce logical conditions in our model building.

As a simple example of binary variables, consider the following scenario: A large construction is budgeting resources for their next fiscal year, and they are considering ten potential projects. Each project has an expected return, an expected investment, and an expected labor requirement. The investment budget is limited to $12M, and the available labor is 100K hours. Details are as follows:

Potential Project	Expected Return ($M)	Expected Inv. ($M)	Expected Labor (K hours)
1	10	2.5	18
2	8	2	13
3	12	2.8	20
4	6	1.2	5
5	4	1	4
6	15	5	22
7	12	3	16
8	9	2	6

TABLE 5-7. POTENTIAL PROJECTS

Additionally, no more than 5 projects are to be pursued, so as to make the high-level project management details as reasonable as possible.

It is desired, of course, that expected revenue be maximized, while simultaneously adhering to the budgets for investment expenditure and labor availability, along with the limit of five projects pursued.

In order to formulate this problem, we define a type of decision variable called "y_i," which takes on a value of either zero or one. Mathematically, we state the following:

$$y_i = 1 \text{ if project i is pursued; 0 otherwise} \qquad \text{EQ 5-21}$$

This means that if a project is not pursued, the binary variable takes on a value of zero, and from a mathematical standpoint, "disappears." Otherwise, if a project is pursued, and it's revenue, expense, labor and pursuance are added accordingly. This results in the following objective function:

$$\text{Max: } 10y_1 + 8y_2 + 12y_3 + 6y_4 + 4y_5 + 15y_6 + 12y_7 + 9y_8 \qquad \text{EQ 5-22}$$

Subject to the following constraints:

$$2.5y_1 + 2y_2 + 2.8y_3 + 1.2y_4 + 1y_5 + 5y_6 + 3y_7 + 2y_8 \leq 12 \qquad \text{EQ 5-23}$$
$$\text{(Budget Limit)}$$

$$18y_1 + 13y_2 + 20y_3 + 5y_4 + 4y_5 + 22y_6 + 16y_7 + 6y_8 \leq 100 \qquad \text{EQ 5-24}$$
$$\text{(Labor Limit)}$$

$$y_1 + y_2 + y_3 + y_4 + y_5 + y_6 + y_7 + y_8 \leq 5 \text{ (Project Limit)} \qquad \text{EQ 5-25}$$

This model can easily be incorporated into Excel. The only nuance here is that the binary decision variables ($y_1 - y_8$) be characterized as binary variables. This is shown in Figure 5-6.

From Figure 5-6, we learn that Projects 1, 3, 4, 7 and 8 should be selected, and will provide an expected revenue of $49M. $11.5M will have been expended, 65K labor hours will have been used, and 5 projects will have been pursued – all of these values have complied with the constraints.

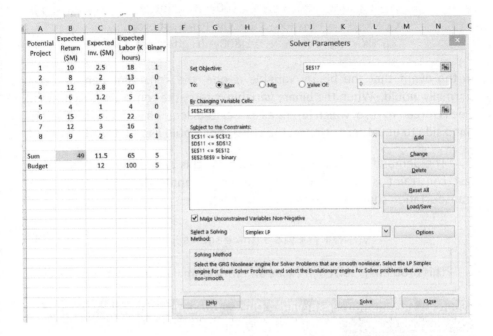

FIGURE 5-6. PROJECT PLANNING PROBLEM

In the above example, we essentially gave ourselves to the ability to use an on/off switch for our decision variables – projects specifically. We can also exploit binary variables to do the same to constraints. If we revisit our transportation problem from Section 5.4.2, we see that we transport from four sources to five destinations. Or more generally, we ship from n possible sources to m possible destinations. With binary variables, we have the ability to use a subset of n if we desire.

We will re-visit the transportation problem example above, and now mandate that at-most, three sources can be used. This type of problem is referred to as a "Fixed-Charge Problem." To solve, we keep all of the decision variables that we previously defined. In addition, we now define a new set of binary variables, that is follows:

$$y_i = 1 \text{ if source is used; } 0 \text{ otherwise} \qquad \text{EQ 5-26}$$

The supply constraints are now as follows:

71

$$x_{11} + x_{12} + x_{13} + x_{14} + x_{15} \leq 1{,}800y_1 \text{ (Winston-Salem)}$$
$$x_{21} + x_{22} + x_{23} + x_{24} + x_{25} \leq 1{,}800y_2 \text{ (Charlotte)} \qquad \text{EQ 5-27}$$
$$x_{31} + x_{32} + x_{33} + x_{34} + x_{35} \leq 1{,}800y_3 \text{ (Greensboro)}$$
$$x_{41} + x_{42} + x_{43} + x_{44} + x_{45} \leq 1{,}800y_4 \text{ (High Point)}$$

In the event that the binary variable is one, the constraint behaves as it normally would. When the binary variable is zero, the constraint's right-hand side is forced to zero, which forces all associated decision variables on the left-hand side to equal zero. Hence, the constraint would essentially "disappear."

The demand constrains do not change in this type of formulation. One last constraint is needed to complete the formulation, which limits the transportation sources to three. This is as follows:

$$y_1 + y_2 + y_3 + y_4 \leq 3 \text{ (three source limit)} \qquad \text{EQ 5-28}$$

This problem is solved in Excel, and the optimal distribution is as follows:

Source \ Destination	Asheville	Duck	Durham	Gastonia	Raleigh
Winston-Salem	0	0	0	0	0
Charlotte	800	0	0	900	0
Greensboro	0	300	1,000	0	200
High Point	0	0	0	0	1,800

TABLE 5 8. OPTIMAL DISTRIBUTION FOR FIXED-CHARGE PROBLEM

The minimized cost is $39,500. It should be noted that Winston-Salem is not a distribution source. There are only three distribution sources, which adheres to the new constraint. It should also be noted that the minimized cost here is inferior to the minimized cost of the earlier transportation problem ($37,900). This should not be surprising – a constraint has been added, subsequently reducing our ability to find the "best" solution.

5.6 Conclusions

Linear programming is a powerful tool in the world of Quantitative Analysis. We build models to assist us in making optimal decisions. This enhances the competitive position of the organization. Optimization models are prevalent in today's world. UPS, FedEx, the US Postal Service, airlines, and railway systems, public utilities are always trying to make optimal decisions regarding the large-scale and complex variety of services they provide.

Linear Programming is the introductory building block to the larger field of "Operations Research," which came into existence during the Industrial Revolution of the early Twentieth Century. At this point in time, economies of scale increased to the point where it was deemed important to pursue all possible gains in efficiency.

Unlike statistics, where a data set is analyzed, Linear Programming essentially starts with a "blank piece of paper" and are asked to build a model to optimize something – this is both intimidating and complicated. It only gets easier with experience.

As stated, Linear Programming is the first step into Operations Research. Subsequent important topics include nonlinear optimization, network optimization and optimal decision-making in the presence of uncertainly.

5.7 Problems

1. The owner of a ranch is trying to determine how to blend two types of animal feed. For the purposes of this exercise, we will call these Feed A and Feed B. Feed A costs \$0.50/pound, while Feed B costs \$0.75/pound. These two animal feeds contain five essential ingredients which need to be present to some degree in the feed mixture. Details of these five essential ingredients, along with their minimum daily requirements are shown below:

Ingredient	Feed A	Feed B	Min Daily Req. (Pounds)
1	20%	25%	30
2	30%	10%	50
3	0%	30%	20
4	24%	15%	60
5	10%	20%	40

    For example, one pound of Feed A contains 0.24 pounds of Ingredient 4, while one pound of Feed B contains 0.15 pounds of Ingredient 4, and the feed mixture must yield at least 60 pounds of Ingredient 4 each day. How should Feed A and Feed B should be mixed such that the total daily cost is minimized subject to the minimum ingredient rules stated above? Formulate and solve as a mathematical programming problem.

2. MetalCo desires to blend a new alloy of 40% tin, 35% zinc, and 25% lead from five available ores having the following properties and costs:

Property	Ore 1	Ore 2	Ore 3	Ore 4	Ore 5
Tin %	60%	25%	45%	20%	50%
Zinc %	10%	15%	45%	50%	40%
Lead %	30%	60%	10%	30%	10%
Cost ($/#)	22	20	25	24	27

For example, one pound of Ore 4 yields 20% tin, 50% zinc, and 30% lead, and costs $24/pound. Your job is to find the minimum cost formulation of these five ores such that the alloy requirement is met. At least 50 pounds of each ore must be used. Formulate and solve as a mathematical programming problem.

3. I have promised a friend that I would copy the Psychedelic Furs' "Forever Now" album for them. Unfortunately, my friend does not have a CD player in their car – just a cassette tape player. Because of this, I need to put music on Side 1 of the tape, and music on Side 2 of the tape. My friend has asked that the total length of the songs be "balanced" as much as possible. By "balanced," my friend means that the total song duration on Side 1 be as close as possible to the total song duration on Side 2. The ten songs, (and their associated durations) that comprise the album are as follows:

Track #	Song	Min	Sec
1	Forever Now	5	37
2	Love My Way	3	35
3	Goodbye	3	56
4	Only You and I	4	26
5	Sleep Comes Down	3	52
6	President Gas	5	21
7	Run and Run	3	49
8	Danger	2	39
9	No Easy Street	4	9
10	Yes I Do	3	54

For example, if Songs 1 – 5 are on Side 1, the music duration will be 1286 sec, while Songs 6 – 10 will then be on Side 2, for a duration of 1192 sec, resulting in a time difference of 94 sec between the two sides. We wish to minimize this time difference. Formulate and solve as a linear programming problem.

4. Ray Bob's Oil Company (RayBobOCo) blends two types of fuel: regular and premium. These fuels are made by blending gasoline and alcohol. RayBobOCo can buy up to 100,000 barrels of gasoline/week at a cost of $80/barrel, and up to 12,000 barrels of alcohol at $94/barrel. Each barrel is equivalent to 55 gallons. Regular is made by blending nine parts of gasoline to one part alcohol. Premium is a blend of 87% gasoline and 13% alcohol. One gallon of regular sells for $2.65, while each gallon of premium sells for $2.83. The market demands at least 600,000 gallons of premium per week, and at least 1 million gallons of regular/week. Additionally, there must be at least twice as much regular produced as compared to premium. Assume that everything produced will be immediately sold. How should RayBobOCo proceed such that their profits are maximized? Formulate as a mathematical programming problem and solve.

5. A company processes coal in northeast Ohio. They grade coal into three groups: Grades A, B and C. They net a profit of $10 for each ton of Grade A, $7.5 for each ton of Grade B, $4 for each ton of Grade C. Each ton of Grade A coal requires 5 hours of processing labor and 1 hour of packaging labor. Each ton of Grade B coal requires 4 hours of processing labor and 0.75 hours of packaging labor. Each ton of Grade C coal requires 3 hours of processing labor and 0.2 hours of packaging labor. There are 100 hours of processing labor available for the next planning period, and there are 200 hours of packaging labor available for the next planning period. Grade A coal can be no more than 50% of the product mix, and Grade C must be at least 20% of the product mix. Processing fractional tons of coal is permitted. How should to the company proceed, in terms of how much of each type of coal to process, such that their profits are maximized? Formulate and solve as a mathematical programming model.

6. Billy's Trucking company specializes in shipping hazardous waste products from four sources (Bangor [Maine], Detroit, El Paso and

Oakland) to four different disposal locations (Berkeley, Boulder, Eugene, Madison). Each of these three sources has generated a quantity of waste requiring disposal (in tons). Each of the four disposal locations has a limited capacity (in tons). Each source / disposal location has a per-unit shipping cost in $/ton. Below is the pricing schedule for each source / destination combination:

	Berkeley	Boulder	Eugene	Madison	Req.
Bangor	75	55	80	40	175
Detroit	65	45	70	12	500
El Paso	50	40	60	42	125
Oakland	6	30	25	45	200
Cap.	800	1100	1200	900	

How should the hazardous waste be transported in a minimum-cost fashion? Formulate and solve as a mathematical programming problem.

7. Re-formulate Problem 6 so that only three disposal sites are permitted.

8. Re-formulated Problem 6 so that only two disposal sites are permitted.

9. Re-formulate Problem 6 so that only one disposal site is permitted.

10. Al, Billy, Cal, Dina, and Eddy are super-salespersons – they can sell anything. Although they have different personalities, they all share the characteristic of being able to sell their company's products. These five sales-persons need to be assigned to different territories. Given their personalities and cultural differences, the matrix below show the estimated sales revenues for each possible territorial assignment. These assignment revenues are as follows:

	East	Northeast	Plains	Southeast	West
Al	100	95	83	85	95
Billy	125	115	110	150	120
Cal	100	105	120	110	115
Dina	105	125	120	95	110
Eddy	110	110	115	85	115

Assign each of these super-salespersons into a territory such that total expected revenue is maximized.

11. A candidate running for the US Senate needs to visit five cities in North Carolina before the election. These five cities are: Asheville,

Charlotte, Greensboro, Raleigh and Wilmington. The candidate needs to return to the same city from which they departed, and must do so in a minimum distance fashion. Using the distance table below (in miles), formulate and solve as a mathematical programming problem.

	Ashe.	Char.	Greens.	Ral.	Wilm.
Asheville	x	131	172	247	332
Charlotte	131	x	92	166	198
Greensboro	172	92	x	76	208
Raleigh	247	166	76	x	130
Wilmington	332	198	208	130	x

12. The Sikafoos Brothers own a construction company, and are planning ahead for the next fiscal year. At present, they are considering ten potential projects. Each potential project has an expected revenue and expected cost. These potential projects are below:

Project	Expected Revenue	Expected Cost
1	$2.2M	$0.6M
2	$1.5M	$0.5M
3	$3M	$1.1M
4	$2.5M	$0.75M
5	$4M	$1M
6	$1.5M	$0.8M
7	$2.3M	$0.7M
8	$5M	$2.75M
9	$1M	$0.3M
10	$2.2M	$1M

The Sikafoos Brothers have a project budget of $5.5M for the next fiscal year. In addition to the limited budget, there are a few other rules that must be followed: Either Project 7 or Project 8 must be chosen, but not both. If Project 3 is chosen, Project 4 must also be chosen. Project 1 and Project 9 must share the same fate – either they will both be chosen, nor neither will be chosen. Your job is to formulated and solve such that total expected revenue is maximized.

13. The Barletto Brothers run a small steel furnace operation. They convert iron ore, scrap metal and refined iron into ingots. They produce two types of ingots: standard and premium. The standard

ingots sell for \$1,000/ton, while the premium ingots sell for \$1,200/ton. They purchase the raw materials with the following prices: iron ore is purchased for \$150/ton, scrap metal is purchased for \$250/ton, while refined iron is purchased for \$600 per ton. For the next planning period, there is an availability of 30 tons of iron ore, 25 tons of scrap metal and 30 tons of refined iron. The standard steel is limited to 25% iron ore, limited to 55% scrap metal, and must be at least 40% refined iron. The premium steel is limited to 18% iron ore, limited to 50% scrap metal and must be at least 45% refined iron. Due to customer contracts, the Standard Steel must be at least 30% of the product-mix. Assume demand for both standard and premium steel to be unlimited. Formulate and solve a mathematical programming model such that net profit is maximized.

This page intentionally left blank.

Made in the USA
Monee, IL
29 September 2023